FISH

FISH

JOANNA FARROW

Bounty
BOOKS

First published in Great Britain in 2007 by Hamlyn,
a division of Octopus Publishing Group Ltd

This edition published in 2011 by Bounty Books,
a division of Octopus Publishing Group Ltd
Endeavour House, 189 Shaftesbury Avenue,
London WC2H 8JY
www.octopusbooks.co.uk

An Hachette UK Company
www.hachette.co.uk

ISBN: 978-0-753722-82-4

A CIP catalogue record for this book is available
from the British Library.

Printed and bound in China

Notes

Both metric and imperial measurements have been given in all recipes. Use one set of measurements only, and not a mixture of both.

Standard level spoon measurements are used in all recipes.
1 tablespoon = one 15 ml spoon
1 teaspoon = one 5 ml spoon

This book includes dishes made with nuts and nut derivatives. It is advisable for those with known allergic reactions to nuts and nut derivatives and those who may be potentially vulnerable to these allergies, such as pregnant and nursing mothers, invalids, the elderly, babies and children, to avoid dishes made with nuts and nut oils. It is also prudent to check the labels of pre-prepared ingredients for the possible inclusion of nut derivatives.

Ovens should be preheated to the specified temperature. If using a fan-assisted oven, follow the manufacturer's instructions for adjusting the time and the temperature.

Contents

Introduction *Among the most inviting aspects of fish cooking are that it's so fast and it's incredibly easy. Fabulous dishes can be made from just a few good basic ingredients and, of course, by using the freshest fish available.*

Despite this, fish remains an ingredient that people are often wary of, and they tend, therefore, to try less-adventurous recipes than they might with different cuts of meat or familiar fish. A beady-eyed snapper, staring up from the fish counter, looks a lot trickier to deal with than a chunky piece of succulent, reassuringly recognizable cod.

Today, with the wonderful choice available, and with the depletion and vulnerability of some of our favourite fish, we simply must become more experimental with our choices. There are many underrated, delicious fish that deserve a bit of culinary magic, whether for everyday family meals or for smart suppers with friends. This book aims to inspire both novice fish cooks and those who might be familiar with fish but who are seeking fresh inspiration.

Buying

One of the slightly frustrating aspects of planning a menu that includes fish is that, unless you're cooking a fish that's widely available, you cannot rely on picking up your exact choice as you might when choosing meat. For this reason, it can be worth ordering two or three days in advance or going to the fishmonger armed with a couple of different recipe ideas.

In addition, fish must eaten absolutely fresh, so a good supplier is essential. Search out a reliable fishmonger in your area or go to the supermarket that has the freshest-looking display on its fish counter. Make your selection of the freshest choice (this way, you'll know what additional ingredients you'll need to buy) so that you can do your other shopping while the fishmonger does any preparation for you.

When you are choosing, look for fish with bright eyes – they should not be sunken, dull or cloudy – and a glossy sheen to the skin. The fish, whole or filleted, should look firm and perky rather than limp, grey and ragged. Be particularly careful when you are buying oily fish, such as mackerel, sardines and herrings, because they deteriorate very quickly.

Sustainable fishing

The fluctuations in the availability of fish and the need to support ethical standards in fishing processes mean that as consumers we can make a positive contribution to the future of the fishing industry, primarily in the way we shop for fish. Widen the range of fish you buy – there is, after all, an incredible choice – and be aware of labelling information. This will vary regionally, but does provide useful facts, such as how and where the fish has been caught and whether it has come from a sustainable supply. If you need advice on choosing fish from well-managed, sustainable stocks, ask the fishmonger and refer to the table on page 16, which gives suggestions for fish you can use as alternatives to those that might be in short supply at present.

Storing

As far as possible, and particularly with shellfish, you should aim to cook on the day you buy. For most of us, this isn't always practicable, however, and if the fish is really fresh, it'll be fine for the next day.

As soon as you get the fish home, gut it (if this has not already been done) and do any other 'messy' preparation, such as scaling. Quickly rinse the whole fish or fillets, removing any traces of blood, but do not soak the fish in water, or you'll end up diluting the flavour. Remove all packaging from prepared fish. Put the fish in a shallow dish, cover it very loosely with clingfilm and store it in the bottom half of the refrigerator.

Shellfish, such as mussels, clams, scallops and oysters, should be cleaned and chilled until you are ready to cook that same day. Cooked shellfish can be stored overnight.

Freezing

Freeze fish with caution. Some raw fish, such as monkfish, salmon and sole, freezes quite well, but other types, including plaice, sea bass, snapper and oily fish, do not. Only freeze fish that is very fresh and keep it for the short term only. A fish that has been in the freezer for three months can end up with a spongy, tough, watery texture.

Preparing fish

Much of the fish bought in supermarkets and from fishmongers comes ready for cooking, leaving you with little preparation. A good fishmonger will also prepare fish for you – gutting or filleting, for example – but if it's a fiddly task, give a little notice so that it can be ready and waiting for you. Don't forget to keep the bones and trimmings for making fish stock (see page 17). It's incredibly easy to do, doesn't take long and makes a huge difference to finished dishes. Once made, fish stock freezes well. The basics of preparing fish are described below, just in case you're presented with a whole fish.

Trimming

If you're serving a whole fish, it's worth cutting off the fins with kitchen scissors, particularly if you have a spiky fish, such as snapper or bass. Leave the tail intact.

Scaling

Not all whole fish will need scaling. Those with very smooth skin, such as mackerel, herring, plaice and lemon sole, do not – test by gently running your fingers from tail to head. Others, such as sea bass, snapper, bream and Dover sole, definitely do.

Scaling can be slightly messy because the scales have a tendency to fly across the room, but they can be controlled if you scale the fish in the sink, inside a carrier bag or wrapped in greaseproof paper, so that you contain as many of the scales as possible. Scrape the fish from tail to head by running a thick-bladed knife close to the skin. Turn the fish over and repeat on the other side. Rinse the fish under cold running water.

Skinning

Whether you serve filleted fish with skin or not is a matter of personal taste and often depends on the recipe. A chunky fillet of pan-fried cod or bass looks and tastes good with skin attached, but you will need to remove the skin if you are cutting the fish into chunks for a casserole or curry.

Lay each fillet, skin side down, on a chopping board and hold the tail end with one hand. Slip a knife between the flesh and the skin and work along the fillet, using a sawing action and keeping the knife close to the skin to avoid wastage. It sometimes helps to rub your fingers holding the tail end with a little salt to prevent it from slipping from your grasp.

Flat fish sometimes have a black discoloration near the thick end of the fillet. This can be rubbed away with salt.

Skinning a whole flat fish

If you prefer, a whole flat fish can be skinned before grilling, frying or baking. Cut away the fins down either side of the fish using sturdy scissors.

Lift a little piece of skin at the tail end by pushing the knife under the skin so that you can get a grip. Dip your fingers in salt, hold the tail with one hand and give the skin a sharp tug with the other, pulling it in the direction of the head. Trim off at the head end and repeat on the other side.

Gutting

Use a sharp knife to slit open the underside of the fish from the head end down to the end of the cavity. Scrape out as much of the insides as you can. Work over a carrier bag or greasproof paper to make clearing up easier. Rinse the fish under cold running water until it is thoroughly clean, removing any traces of blood.

Filleting a round fish

Lay the fish on a chopping board. Cut through the fillet at the head end through to the backbone. Turn the knife and cut along the back of the fish, slicing the knife closely against one side of the backbone. Continue slicing down the length of the fish, releasing the fillet completely at the tail end. Turn the fish over and repeat on the other side.

Filleting a flat fish

Put the fish flat on the board. Using a long, slender knife, preferably a filleting knife, cut around the head. Make a cut down the centre of the fish, following the line of the backbone. Starting at the head end, slip the knife into the cut and slide it horizontally against the backbone out to the edge of the fish, holding the released part of the fillet with the other hand. Continue removing the fillet until it comes away completely. Keep the knife as close to the bones as possible to avoid wastage. Remove the adjacent fillet in the same way. Turn the fish over and remove the remaining fillets.

Scoring

Scoring not only makes the fish look more attractive when it is grilled, roasted or barbecued, but also helps the flesh to absorb the flavours of a marinade or sauce.

Use a very sharp knife and score the flesh diagonally on each side. You can also make cuts in the other direction to make a criss-cross pattern.

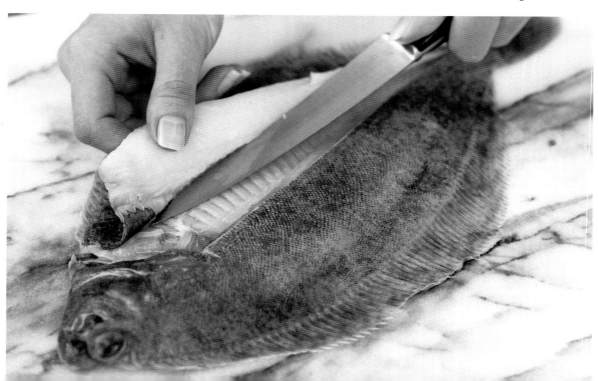

Boning small whole fish

Small whole fish, such as herrings and small mackerel, are much easier to eat once they have been boned. Cut the head off the gutted fish. Open out the underside of the fish on the board so that the skin side is uppermost. Press down firmly along the backbone to release the flesh. You'll feel this happening under the pressure of your thumb. Turn the fish over and pull away the backbone in one go, cutting it at the tail end to release.

Removing stray bones

Most stray bones are found near the head end of filleted fish. Use your fingers to feel where the bones are, and then use a pair of tweezers to get a firm grip on the end of the bone and pull it out firmly.

Boning monkfish

Monkfish has one thick central bone, which can be easily removed by running a knife down one side of the bone to release the fillet. Repeat on the other side of the bone. The fillets usually have a thick membrane around them that, if left on, toughens the fillets during cooking. Gently ease the membrane away with a knife.

Soaking salt cod

When you buy salt cod, choose chunky pieces rather than thin ones that resemble cardboard. Immerse the cod in a large bowl of cold water and leave it to soak for two to three days, changing the water a couple of times each day. The soaking can be done at room temperature, but you might prefer to put it in the refrigerator during very hot weather.

Preparing shellfish and cephalopods
Shellfish doesn't store as well as other types of fish and is best cooked on the day you buy it. Much of the shellfish available now is already cooked, but if you can buy raw and cook it yourself, the results will be far more rewarding. Squid and cuttlefish are cephalopods, a group that also includes octopus.

Clams and cockles
Although these are less gritty and barnacled than mussels (see right), you will still need to check through clams and cockles carefully, discarding any damaged or stubbornly open shells.

Cuttlefish
Cuttlefish have chubbier bodies than those of the squid, and they have a large, flat bone inside the body. This is most easily removed by cutting down the length of the body and discarding the bone along with the other innards. Otherwise, prepare in the same way as squid (see opposite).

Mussels
Wash mussels in cold water to remove all traces of grit. Scrape off any barnacles with a knife and pull away the beards (the seaweed-like threads that the mussels use to cling to rocks and ropes). As you clean them, check that all the shells are intact, discarding any that are cracked or damaged. Any mussels that are open should close when tapped sharply against the side of the sink. Discard any that don't close.

Prawns
Both raw and cooked prawns are prepared by pinching off the heads and then peeling away the

shells. If you are serving prawns in a salad, you might prefer to leave the tails intact, but remove them if you are adding them to other ingredients. Remove the black, thread-like intestine that runs down the back or underside of larger prawns by making a small cut and pulling it away.

Scallops

Scallops are usually bought ready prepared, but they are easy to open if you buy them in their shells. Place them on a chopping board with the flat shell uppermost and insert the blade of a sturdy knife between the two shells on the opposite side to the hinge. Run the knife against the flat top shell so that you can sever the meat from the shell. Discard everything except the coral and white muscle flesh.

Squid

Most squid, which are also called calamari or inkfish, can be bought ready prepared, either as the body tubes alone or cleaned out with the heads popped back in the tubes. Larger squid are also available ready sliced into rings.

If you buy them whole with skin attached, pull away the head and tentacles from the body, then scoop out and discard the contents of the body, including the transparent, plasticky quill. Pull off and discard the inky skin. This usually rubs off very easily with your fingers. The fins on either side of the body can be removed for cooking separately. Remove the tentacles from the head by cutting just in front of the eyes so that they remain in one piece. Discard the heads. If the recipe requires, slice the body into rings. Dry all the pieces thoroughly and chill until ready to cook.

Cooking fish

The fresher the fish, the less you need to do to it to make it taste fabulous. All fish is quick to cook, particularly if you're frying or grilling, so make sure you have any accompaniments ready prepared (or at least planned) so that the fish is not hanging around. Unlike meat, there are no hard and fast rules when it comes to cooking fish, and almost any type of fish can be cooked in any way without the fear of tough or flavourless results. It's more a case of what kind of cooking method you're in the mood for, whether a comforting fish fry-up or an Asian-style, fragrantly steamed fish, for example.

Shallow-frying

Fish can be fried to sear in the flavour before it is added to stews or curries, or just fried for a simple dish. You will need a good-quality, nonstick frying pan, which is essential for getting a crisp skin and for preventing the fish from sticking to the pan.

Shallow-frying gives fish an appetizing golden colour, but take care that you don't overcrowd the pan, which reduces the cooking temperature and steams the fish in its juices. Turn the fish halfway through frying and, if you are serving with it skin on, fry skin side down first.

Grilling

Grilling can be a healthy way to cook fish, but the flavour is usually enhanced by a douching of butter or oil. If you are using a traditional overhead grill, make sure it's really hot before you start cooking. Make deep slashes in the fish (if it's to be served whole) so that the heat can penetrate the fish quickly and speed up cooking. For convenience, line the grill pan with foil and brush it with butter or oil before cooking so that the fish don't stick to the foil.

All fish can be grilled, but flat fish are particularly suitable for this method, and a deliciously fresh sole or plaice can be ready to eat in less than 10 minutes.

Confusingly, the term chargrilling is used to describe both the technique of cooking over coals, as on a barbecue, and also in the small, ridged griddle pans that are used over the stove. No matter which method you use, chargrilling is great for cooking firm-textured, meaty fish, such as tuna, shark and swordfish. Brush the ridges with oil first and make sure the pan is very hot before you add the fish. Turn once during cooking so that you don't spoil the appetizingly seared marks on the fish.

Barbecuing

Most fish can be cooked well and fast on a barbecue. Shellfish are delicious cooked this way, as are steaks of tuna, swordfish and shark. Whole fish, including small flat fish and red mullet, sea bass and snapper, also cook very successfully. Oily fish, particularly sardines and herrings, are perfect for barbecuing and eliminate the problem of lingering fish odours that you get when cooking them indoors.

Remember to brush the rack as well as the fish itself

with olive oil to prevent the fish from sticking. A sprinkling of fresh herbs and seasoning is all that's needed for additional flavour. You can buy fish-shaped presses in various sizes, and these make turning the fish much easier.

Deep-frying

You don't need an electric deep-fat fryer or even a deep-fat fryer fitted with a special basket, although this does make removing the fish – and chips – much easier. An ordinary large, sturdy saucepan will do, and you will need a large slotted spoon. Never fill the pan more than one-third full with oil and make sure you get the oil to the right temperature before adding any food. Use a thermometer if you have one, cooking fish at 180–190°C (350–375°F), or test the temperature by adding a small cube of bread or a drop of batter to the pan. It should sizzle instantly and turn golden in about 30 seconds.

During cooking, keep an eye on the speed of cooking. If you feel that a piece of battered fish is frying too fast, reduce the heat or turn it off altogether.

Roasting

The technique for roasting fish is similar to that for meat – that is, a piece of seasoned fish is cooked at a high temperature. Get the oven really hot before you add the fish, which can be whole or in fillets, and drizzle with oil or butter to keep it moist. After roasting, the pan juices can be swirled with reduced fish stock, wine or cream and made into a creamy sauce.

Baking

Baking can be similar to roasting except that the fish might be cooked more slowly and at a lower temperature. Baked fish is often cooked in liquid – stock or wine – and might include vegetables and herbs.

Steaming

Steamed fish is often thought of as being rather bland, and steaming is usually a technique that is used only when someone is on a strict weight-loss diet! But steamed fish can be far from dull, particularly if it has been marinated in aromatic ingredients, such as ginger, lime, garlic and spices, so that the flavours seep right into the fish.

Fish can be steamed in a bamboo steamer, set over a pan or wok of simmering water, or on a wok rack, tented with foil or a domed lid. Even simpler is to 'oven-steam' fish by laying it on a wire rack in a roasting tin containing a shallow depth of boiled water and covering the whole pan with foil (see, for example, Steamed Bream with Lemon Grass and Ginger on page 87).

Poaching

The traditional method of poaching large whole fish in a court bouillon is not common now, but any pieces of fish lowered into a gently simmering stock or stew is still a form of poaching, as the fish cooks gently in the juices. Keep the pieces of fish quite chunky and make sure the liquid is barely simmering. If it's allowed to boil away frantically, the pieces of fish will quickly fall apart.

For recipes using	you could also try...
ANCHOVIES	Sprats • Sardines • Whitebait
CLAMS	Mussels • Oysters • Cockles • Razor Clams
COD	Pollack • Hoki • Haddock • Coley • Hake • Whiting (large)
CRAYFISH	Langoustines • Prawns (large)
HADDOCK, SMOKED	Smoked Cod • Kippers
HAKE	Cod
HALIBUT	Brill • Turbot
HERRINGS	Mackerel • Pilchards • Sardines
MACKEREL	Sardines • Herrings • Pilchards
MACKEREL, SMOKED	Smoked Eel • Smoked Salmon • Smoked Trout
MONKFISH	Cod
PERCH	Salmon • Trout
PLAICE	Dover Sole • Lemon Sole • Witch Sole • Dab (large) • Flounder
PRAWNS	Scallops • Langoustine (Dublin Bay Prawns) • Scampi • Shrimps
RED MULLET	Tilapia • Sea Bream • Sea Bass
RED SNAPPER	Sea Bream • Red Mullet • Red Bream
SALMON	Trout • Salmon Trout • Sea Trout
SARDINES	Herrings • Pilchards • Mackerel (small)
SEA BASS	John Dory • Turbot • Brill
SEA BREAM	Red Bream • Red Mullet • Red Snapper
SQUID (CALAMARI, INKFISH)	Cuttlefish • Octopus
SWORDFISH	Ray • Shark
TROUT, SMOKED	Smoked Mackerel • Smoked Eel
TUNA	Shark • Swordfish • Bonito • Mahi Mahi
TURBOT	Halibut • Brill

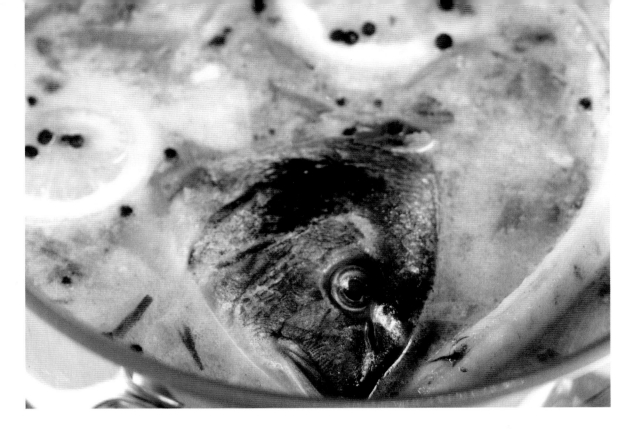

Fish stock

You can use almost any white fish trimmings in this stock, including the heads, tails and bones. Shellfish trimmings, such as prawn heads and shells, can also be used. Avoid oily fish, which has too strong a flavour and will give a greasy result.

PREPARATION TIME: 5 minutes
COOKING TIME: 30 minutes
MAKES: about 900 ml (1½ pints)

25 g (1 oz) butter
1 onion or several shallots, chopped
2 celery sticks, chopped
1 kg (2 lb) white fish and shellfish trimmings (see above)
150 ml (¼ pint) dry white wine
several parsley stalks
several lemon slices
1 teaspoon black peppercorns

1 Melt the butter in a large, heavy-based saucepan and gently fry the vegetables until they are softened but not browned.

2 Add the fish and shellfish trimmings, wine, parsley, lemon and peppercorns and top up with 1 litre (1¾ pints) cold water. Bring almost to the boil, then reduce the heat and simmer gently for 25 minutes.

3 Strain through a sieve and leave to cool. Cover and chill for up to 24 hours.

Creamy béchamel sauce

This rich and creamy sauce is an essential requirement in fish pies and crêpes. Alternatively, use one of the variations below and pour over grilled or steamed white fish for a quick and easy – but delicious – supper dish.

PREPARATION TIME: 10 minutes, plus infusing

COOKING TIME: 10 minutes

MAKES: about 500 ml (17 fl oz)

200 ml (7 fl oz) milk

2 bay leaves

1 small onion, quartered

1 teaspoon black peppercorns

50 g (2 oz) butter

40 g (1½ oz) plain flour

300 ml (½ pint) single cream

freshly grated nutmeg

salt and pepper

1 Put the milk in a saucepan with the bay leaves, onion and peppercorns. Bring almost to the boil, then remove from the heat, leave to infuse for 15 minutes. Strain through a sieve.

2 Melt the butter in a heavy-based saucepan. Tip in the flour and stir in quickly. Cook gently for 1 minute.

3 Remove from the heat and stir in the strained milk, then the cream. Return to the heat and cook gently, stirring continuously, until thickened and smooth. Season to taste with nutmeg and salt and pepper.

Rich cheese sauce Stir in 150 g (5 oz) grated Cheddar or Gruyère cheese, or use 125 g (4 oz) of either cheese and add 25 g (1 oz) grated Parmesan.

Parsley sauce Once the milk is strained, blend it in a food processor with 15 g (½ oz) curly parsley, tough stalks removed. Alternatively, finely chop the parsley and add to the thickened sauce.

Rouille
This hot, fiery sauce is usually served separately at the table for swirling into fish soups, such as Soupe de Poissons (see page 30). It's also good for 'hotting up' fish stews and as an alternative to aïoli for accompanying Salt Cod Fritters (see page 116). It keeps well in the refrigerator for several days in a tightly sealed container.

PREPARATION TIME: 5 minutes
MAKES: 175 ml (6 fl oz)

1 hot red chilli, deseeded and sliced
4 garlic cloves, chopped
1 egg yolk
25 g (1 oz) breadcrumbs
150 ml (¼ pint) olive oil
salt

1 Blend the chilli, garlic, egg yolk, breadcrumbs and a little salt in a food processor or blender to make a thick paste, scraping down any mixture that clings to the side of the bowl.

2 With the machine running, gradually drizzle in the oil until the mixture is the consistency of a thin mayonnaise. Turn into a dish, cover and chill until needed.

Tip If the Rouille separates after step 2, whizz in a few drops of hot water. Alternatively, put another egg yolk in the cleaned food processor or blender and blend the separated Rouille.

Mayonnaise
Using olive oil in mayonnaise gives the best results, although you can use half olive oil and half sunflower or groundnut oil for a milder flavour. It keeps well in the refrigerator, covered, for a couple of days.

PREPARATION TIME: 10 minutes
MAKES: 300 ml (½ pint)

2 egg yolks
½ teaspoon Dijon mustard
250 ml (8 fl oz) olive oil
1–2 tablespoons lemon juice or white wine vinegar
salt and pepper

1 Put the egg yolks, mustard and a little seasoning in a food processor or blender and blend briefly.

2 With the machine running, very slowly add the oil in a thin trickle until thickened. (Once the mixture has thickened, you can start to add the oil more quickly.)

3 Lightly blend in enough lemon juice or vinegar to give a bit of tang and check the seasoning. Turn into a bowl, cover and chill until ready to serve.

Aïoli Some Mediterranean recipes use several cloves of garlic in this mayonnaise, but the flavour can be overpowering. Start by adding one plump garlic clove, crushed, at step 1. You can always add more garlic if you prefer a stronger flavour. Keep, well covered, in the refrigerator.

Crème fraîche and herb mayonnaise Add 100 g (3½ oz) crème fraîche and 4 tablespoons chopped herbs (such as chives, dill, parsley, tarragon or coriander) to the finished mayonnaise.

Garlic, rosemary and caper butter
Almost any herbs and aromatics can be blended with butter to make a delicious topping for most grilled, steamed or baked fish. Store it in the refrigerator for several days or shape it into a log, wrap it in greaseproof paper and freeze.

PREPARATION TIME: 5 minutes
SERVES: 4–6

100 g (3½ oz) lightly salted butter, softened
2 teaspoons finely chopped rosemary
1 tablespoon chopped parsley
1 garlic clove, crushed
finely grated rind of 1 lemon
1 tablespoon capers, rinsed, drained and chopped
pepper

1 Put the butter in a bowl with the rosemary, parsley, garlic, lemon rind, capers and plenty of pepper and beat well until thoroughly combined.

2 Turn into a small bowl, cover and chill until ready to serve.

Variation Omit the capers and use other herbs, such as chervil, chives, tarragon, coriander or dill, instead of the rosemary and parsley.

Roasted tomato sauce

This sauce, a fabulous partner to so many fish dishes, is worth making only if really ripe, flavoursome fresh tomatoes are available; otherwise, use a couple of cans of chopped tomatoes.

PREPARATION TIME: 10 minutes

COOKING TIME: 50 minutes

MAKES: 750 ml (1¼ pints)

1 kg (2 lb) very ripe tomatoes

4 tablespoons olive oil

1 teaspoon caster sugar

1 onion, finely chopped

4 garlic cloves, crushed

2 tablespoons chopped oregano

salt and pepper

1 Halve the tomatoes and arrange them, cut sides up, in a large, shallow, ovenproof dish or roasting tin. Drizzle with 2 tablespoons of the oil, the sugar and seasoning. Roast in a preheated oven, 200°C (400°F), Gas Mark 6, for 40 minutes or until the tomatoes are soft and beginning to colour.

2 Gently fry the onion in the remaining oil in a saucepan for about 10 minutes or until it is soft, adding the garlic for the last couple of minutes. Blend the tomatoes in a food processor or blender and add to the pan with the oregano.

3 Cook gently for 5–10 minutes or until slightly thickened. Check the seasoning and serve.

Hollandaise sauce
Rich and buttery, but with a light tang, a blanket of hollandaise sauce over a succulent piece of white fish or salmon is one of the loveliest dishes. The sauce keeps for no more than about 30 minutes before serving – keep it covered with a lid over the bowl of hot water and with the heat turned off.

PREPARATION TIME: 10 minutes

COOKING TIME: 10 minutes   **SERVES:** 6

2 tablespoons white wine vinegar

1 bay leaf

½ teaspoon black peppercorns

3 egg yolks

200 g (7 oz) unsalted butter, softened and cut into 1 cm (½ inch) cubes

salt and pepper

1 Heat the vinegar, bay leaf and peppercorns together with 1 tablespoon water in a small saucepan until bubbling and reduced by half.

2 Heat a larger saucepan containing a depth of 5 cm (2 inches) water until simmering. Strain the vinegar mixture into a large bowl, add the egg yolks and whisk lightly to combine.

3 Place the large bowl over the pan of simmering water and whisk in a cube of butter until it melts into the sauce. Keep whisking in the remaining butter, a piece at a time, until the mixture is thick and glossy. Season to taste and check the flavour, adding a dash more vinegar if needed.

Hollandaise sauce with herbs Fresh herbs, such as parsley, dill, tarragon, fennel or chives, can be added to the basic sauce. Use 2–3 tablespoons, finely chopped, and whisk in with the butter.

Crushed minted peas
A compulsory accompaniment to the best fish and chips, this is the homemade answer to the pale, sloppy pea purée that is often sold to partner bought fish and chips.

PREPARATION TIME: 10 minutes

COOKING TIME: 5 minutes   **SERVES:** 4–6

400 g (13 oz) fresh peas, shelled

several sprigs of mint

25 g (1 oz) butter

2 tablespoons crème fraîche

salt and pepper

1 Cook the peas with the mint in a large saucepan of boiling water for about 5 minutes or until very tender. Drain and return to the pan, discarding the mint.

2 Stir in the butter and crème fraîche and use a potato masher to crush the peas roughly. Season to taste with salt and pepper and reheat gently.

Tip Fresh peas have a good texture and flavour, but you can use frozen peas instead if necessary.

Marsh samphire

This vegetable, which is sometimes sold in fishmongers, makes a fitting accompaniment to fish dishes, particularly white fish. It is firm-textured, slightly salty and easy to cook.

PREPARATION TIME: 5 minutes
COOKING TIME: 5 minutes   **SERVES:** 4

225 g (7½ oz) marsh samphire
25 g (1 oz) butter
pepper

1 Trim the woody stem ends from the samphire and wash it in several changes of cold water. Drain.

2 Cook in a saucepan of boiling water for 4–5 minutes or until tender. Drain, return to the pan and dot with the butter. Season with plenty of pepper.

Buttery celeriac mash

Similar to celery in flavour, celeriac makes a delicious mash, which is perfect with pan-fried or baked fish dishes, particularly when there are lots of buttery juices. For a good, 'mashy' consistency, it's best combined with some floury potato.

PREPARATION TIME: 15 minutes

COOKING TIME: 20 minutes   **SERVES:** 4–6

1 kg (2 lb) celeriac

500 g (1 lb) floury potatoes, cut into chunks

4 tablespoons milk

40 g (1½ oz) butter

salt and pepper

1 Cut away the knobbly skin from the celeriac. Chop the flesh into chunks similar in size to the potatoes. Put both vegetables in a saucepan and cover with cold water. Bring to the boil, then reduce the heat and simmer gently for 15–20 minutes or until very tender.

2 Drain well and return to the pan. Add the milk, butter and a little seasoning and mash well until smooth. Reheat gently and serve.

Chunky potato chips

This is the no-fuss version of traditional chips. They are simple to make – you can pop them in the oven and forget about them (unlike fried chips) – and are a good accompaniment to pan-fried, baked or grilled fish.

PREPARATION TIME: 10 minutes

COOKING TIME: 50 minutes   **SERVES:** 4

1 kg (2 lb) baking potatoes

150 ml (¼ pint) mild olive oil or groundnut oil

1 teaspoon ground paprika

1 teaspoon celery salt

salt and pepper

1 Cut the potatoes into 1 cm (½ inch) slices, then cut each potato slice into chunky chips.

2 Brush a large roasting tin with a little of the oil and heat it in a preheated oven, 220°C (425°F), Gas Mark 7, for 5 minutes.

3 Scatter the chips in the tin, drizzle with the remaining oil and sprinkle with the paprika and celery salt. Mix until well coated. Bake for 45 minutes, turning the chips occasionally, until they are golden. Serve sprinkled with salt and pepper.

Soups and stews

Fish can be used to make a wide range of soups and casseroles, and this section includes traditional dishes from southern Europe and modern versions of North African and Asian recipes. Fish soup can be served as an appetizing starter or, in larger portions and accompanied by fresh, crusty bread, as a meal in its own right. The key to success is to cook these dishes slowly and gently so that the fish retains its flavour and does not disintegrate.

Clam chowder

A kilo of clams provides surprisingly little meat, but the pronounced flavour, combined with the salt pork, makes a rich, hearty soup that's good as a starter or, in larger portions, as a main course.

PREPARATION TIME: 20 minutes

COOKING TIME: 35 minutes   **SERVES:** 4

1 kg (2 lb) clams, cleaned (see page 12)

200 g (7 oz) salt pork, finely chopped

1 large onion, chopped

15 g (½ oz) butter

1 tablespoon plain flour

4 tomatoes, skinned and chopped

350 g (11½ oz) potatoes, diced

2 bay leaves

3 tablespoons chopped parsley

2 teaspoons Tabasco sauce

150 ml (¼ pint) single cream

1 Bring 150 ml (¼ pint) water to the boil in a saucepan. Add the clams, cover with a tight-fitting lid and cook for 4–5 minutes or until the shells have opened. Drain, reserving the cooking juices, and discard any that remain closed. Remove the flesh from the shells and chop it into small pieces.

2 Put the pork and onion in a large saucepan with a knob of the butter and fry gently for 10 minutes or until browned. Stir in the remaining butter until melted. Add the flour and cook, stirring, for 1 minute.

3 Add the clam cooking juices and 450 ml (¾ pint) water, the tomatoes, potatoes and bay leaves. Bring just to the boil, then reduce the heat, cover and cook very gently for 15 minutes or until the potatoes are tender.

4 Stir in the clams and parsley and cook very gently for a further 2 minutes. Add the Tabasco sauce and cream, heat through and serve.

Clam chowder

Soupe de poissons

French fish markets sell soupe de poissons, *a selection of small fish, specifically for this classic dish. For equally good results, make up the weight with any of the fish suggested.*

PREPARATION TIME: 40 minutes

COOKING TIME: 45 minutes   **SERVES:** 4

1 kg (2 lb) mixed fish (such as small flat fish, snapper, gurnard, skate or conger eel), gutted

1 large onion, roughly chopped

2 carrots, roughly chopped

1 head fennel, chopped

3 garlic cloves

5 tablespoons olive oil

1 bouquet garni

½ teaspoon saffron strands

2 tablespoons tomato purée

salt and pepper

Rouille, to serve (see page 19)

1 Cut the fish into manageable pieces that will fit into the pan. (All parts of the gutted fish are used because they flavour the soup and are strained after cooking, so there is no need to remove heads, fins and so on.)

2 Put the onion, carrots, fennel, garlic and oil in a large saucepan and fry for 10 minutes or until softened. Add all the fish, the bouquet garni and 1.2 litres (2 pints) water and bring to a simmer. Cook gently, covered, for 30 minutes or until the vegetables are soft and the fish is falling apart. Lift out the bouquet garni.

3 Blend the soup, in batches, in a food processor or blender until smooth. Strain through a coarse sieve into a clean pan and add the saffron and tomato purée. Season to taste.

4 Heat through gently and ladle into bowls. Serve with the Rouille in a separate bowl for stirring in.

Tip If the consistency of the soup is too thin, blend 15 g (½ oz) softened butter to a paste with 15 g (½ oz) plain flour. Whisk the *buerre manié* into the soup, heating gently, until thickened.

Thai mussel soup
This delicious aromatic soup is best served freshly made so that the mussels aren't hanging around for too long. Don't be put off by this – you can have the mussels cleaned and the Thai paste blended so that everything's ready to go.

PREPARATION TIME: 20 minutes
COOKING TIME: 15 minutes   **SERVES:** 4

300 ml (½ pint) Fish Stock (see page 17)

1 kg (2 lb) mussels, cleaned (see page 12)

1 stalk of lemon grass, thinly sliced

50 g (2 oz) fresh root ginger, roughly chopped

3 garlic cloves, roughly chopped

2 shallots, roughly chopped

1 celery stick, chopped

1 small green chilli, deseeded and chopped

25 g (1 oz) fresh coriander

½ teaspoon ground turmeric

2 teaspoons caster sugar

1 tablespoon Thai fish sauce

2 tablespoons lime juice

400 ml (14 fl oz) can coconut milk

chunky bread, to serve

1 Bring the stock to the boil in a large saucepan. Tip in the mussels, cover with a tight-fitting lid and cook for 4–5 minutes or until the mussels have opened. Drain the mussels, reserving the stock. Reserve about a quarter of the mussels in their shells, discarding any unopened ones. Remove the remainder from their shells.

2 Put the lemon grass, ginger, garlic, shallots, celery, chilli, coriander and turmeric in a food processor and blend to a fine paste, scraping down the mixture from the side of the bowl if necessary. Tip into a large saucepan. Add all but a ladleful of the stock and bring to a simmer. Cover and cook gently for 5 minutes.

3 Put the sugar, fish sauce, lime juice, shelled mussels and remaining stock in a food processor and blend until completely smooth.

4 Pour the mixture into the saucepan and add the coconut milk. Heat through until simmering. Arrange little piles of the whole mussels in shallow, warm soup bowls and ladle over the soup. Serve hot with chunky bread.

Shellfish laksa

A laksa is an Asian one-pot dish of seafood and noodles in a spicy coconut broth. This version makes a great supper dish, or you can serve smaller portions as an appetite-stimulating starter.

PREPARATION TIME: 20 minutes

COOKING TIME: 15 minutes   **SERVES:** 4

1 hot red chilli, deseeded and sliced

1 stalk of lemon grass, thinly sliced

1 onion, roughly chopped

50 g (2 oz) fresh root ginger, roughly chopped

50 g (2 oz) unsalted roasted peanuts

4 teaspoons Thai fish sauce

3 tablespoons groundnut oil or mild olive oil

8 shelled scallops, halved if large (see page 13)

½ teaspoon ground turmeric

600 ml (1 pint) Fish Stock (see page 17)

400 ml (14 fl oz) can coconut milk

150 g (5 oz) dried egg noodles

200 g (7 oz) raw peeled prawns

150 g (5 oz) white crabmeat

150 g (5 oz) bean sprouts

15 g (½ oz) fresh coriander, chopped

1 Put the chilli, lemon grass, onion, ginger, peanuts and fish sauce in a food processor and blend to a thick paste.

2 Heat the oil in a large saucepan and gently fry the scallops until they are seared on all sides. Drain with a slotted spoon. Add the paste to the pan and fry gently, stirring, for 5 minutes. Add the turmeric, stock and coconut milk and bring slowly to a simmer.

3 Cook the noodles in a separate saucepan until they are tender, following the instructions on the packet.

4 Meanwhile, stir the prawns and scallops into the broth and cook gently for 3 minutes or until the prawns have turned pink. Stir in the crabmeat, bean sprouts and coriander and cook for 1 minute. Drain the noodles, pile them into serving bowls, top with the laksa and serve.

Shellfish laksa

Portuguese fish stew

You can use almost any white fish in this flexible stew, so take your pick of the freshest and best on offer. Serve with crusty bread for dipping in the delicious juices.

PREPARATION TIME: 25 minutes

COOKING TIME: 45 minutes   **SERVES:** 6

1.5 kg (3 lb) mixed white fish (such as hake, haddock or monkfish fillet, red mullet, shark or swordfish)

400 g (13 oz) cleaned small squid (see page 13)

6 tablespoons olive oil

2 onions, chopped

3 green peppers, deseeded and quartered

4 garlic cloves, finely chopped

750 g (1½ lb) tomatoes, skinned and chopped

800 g (1 lb 10 oz) floury potatoes, cut into chunks

1 glass dry white wine

600 ml (1 pint) Fish Stock (see page 17)

4 tablespoons sun-dried tomato paste

3 bay leaves

25 g (1 oz) chopped fresh coriander

salt and pepper

1 Cut the fish into large chunks, discarding the skin and any bones. (If you're using red mullet, there is no need to remove the skin from the fish.)

2 Slice the squid if more than about 5 cm (2 inches) long and reserve the tentacles if liked.

3 Heat half the oil in a large, heavy-based saucepan and gently fry the onions and green peppers until softened. Add the garlic, tomatoes, potatoes, wine, stock, tomato paste, bay leaves and remaining oil and simmer, uncovered, for 30 minutes.

4 Lower the white fish into the stew and cook gently for 5 minutes. Add the squid and coriander and cook for a further 5 minutes or until all the fish is cooked through. Season to taste and serve in large, shallow bowls.

Portuguese fish stew

Bouillabaisse *In a traditional bouillabaisse, the fish is drained, and then the broth and fish are served separately. This simplified version serves the whole lot in a bowl, keeping the flavours intensely mingled. Spoon aïoli or rouille (or both) on to the toast for floating on the soup and absorbing all the fabulous flavours.*

PREPARATION TIME: 25 minutes

COOKING TIME: 45 minutes   SERVES: 4–6

1 kg (2 lb) mixed fish fillets (such as monkfish, haddock, cod, hake, mullet, bream, gurnard and conger eel)

4 tablespoons olive oil

1 large onion, chopped

2 small leeks, sliced

2 pared strips orange rind

2 celery sticks, sliced

4 garlic cloves, sliced

1 teaspoon saffron threads

2 tablespoons Pernod (optional)

400 g (13 oz) tomatoes, skinned and chopped

8 shelled scallops (see page 13)

250 g (8 oz) whole raw prawns, crayfish or langoustines

salt and pepper

To serve:

toasted baguette slices

Aïoli (see page 20) or Rouille (see page 19)

1 Cut the fish into small portions. The skin can be removed from the white fish, but leave it on red mullet (if used) for colour. Heat the oil in a large saucepan and gently fry the onion and leeks for 5 minutes.

2 Add the orange rind, celery and garlic and fry for a further 2 minutes. Stir in the saffron and Pernod (if used) and cover with 1.5 litres (2½ pints) water. Bring to the boil, then reduce the heat and simmer gently for 20 minutes.

3 Lower the fish and tomatoes into the pan and cook briefly until opaque. Add the scallops and shellfish and cook for a further 10 minutes.

4 Use a large slotted spoon to ladle the fish and vegetables into warm soup bowls. Boil the broth to reduce it slightly, season to taste and ladle it over the fish. Serve with the toasted baguette slices topped with Aïoli or Rouille.

Squid, chickpea and pepper stew
Squid can sometimes be bought already cut into rings, ready for frying in batter. You can also use the rings more interestingly in this colourful, fresh-tasting stew.

PREPARATION TIME: 20 minutes

COOKING TIME: 25 minutes   **SERVES:** 2–3

1 tablespoon plain flour

400 g (13 oz) squid rings (see page 13)

4 tablespoons olive oil

1 head fennel, chopped

2 green peppers, deseeded and sliced

2 garlic cloves, crushed

1 tablespoon chopped oregano

600 ml (1 pint) Fish Stock (see page 17)

400 g (13 oz) can chickpeas, rinsed and drained

squeeze of lemon juice

8 cherry tomatoes, halved

salt and pepper

1 Season the flour and use it to dust the squid rings. Heat the oil in a large saucepan and gently fry the fennel and peppers for 5 minutes. Add the garlic and oregano and fry for a further 5 minutes.

2 Add the squid to the pan and fry for 5 minutes or until they puff into rings.

3 Stir in the stock and chickpeas and bring to a simmer. Cook gently, covered, for 10 minutes.

4 Add the lemon juice and the tomatoes and season to taste. Cook for a further minute and serve.

Moroccan fish tagine
This spicy, aromatic stew can be made using chunky fillets of almost any white fish. For best results, the pieces need to be large so that they don't disintegrate during the slow cooking.

PREPARATION TIME: 15 minutes

COOKING TIME: 55 minutes   **SERVES:** 4

750 g (1½ lb) firm white fish fillets (such as cod, sea bass or monkfish), skinned

½ teaspoon cumin seeds

½ teaspoon coriander seeds

6 cardamom pods

4 tablespoons olive oil

2 small onions, thinly sliced

2 garlic cloves, crushed

¼ teaspoon ground turmeric

1 cinnamon stick

40 g (1½ oz) sultanas

25 g (1 oz) pine nuts, lightly toasted

150 ml (¼ pint) Fish Stock (see page 17)

finely grated rind of 1 lemon, plus 1 tablespoon juice

salt and pepper

chopped parsley, to garnish

1 Cut the fish into large chunks, each about 5 cm (2 inches) square, and season.

2 Use a pestle and mortar to crush the cumin and coriander seeds and cardamom pods. Discard the cardamom pods, leaving the seeds.

3 Heat the oil in a large, shallow frying pan and gently fry the onions for 6–8 minutes until golden. Add the garlic and the spices and fry gently, stirring, for 2 minutes. Add the fish pieces, turning them until they are coated in the oil. Transfer the fish and onions to an ovenproof casserole dish and scatter with the sultanas and pine nuts.

4 Add the stock and lemon rind and juice to the frying pan and bring to the boil. Pour the mixture around the fish, cover with a lid and bake in a preheated oven, 160°C (325°F), Gas Mark 3, for 40 minutes.

Moroccan fish tagine

Snacks, salads and light meals

Fish is often used in starters because it's not too rich and lends itself to small portions, mingling with stimulating flavours that whet the appetite for what's to follow. The recipes in this chapter include classics such as Potted Prawns, as well as tapas-style tasters and crispy baked pastries. Most of the recipes make equally enticing light meals, especially when served with a leafy salad and a well-flavoured bread.

Potted prawns with fennel pittas
Submerged in mildly spiced, garlicky butter, these little pots of freshly cooked prawns are a fabulous 'make-ahead' starter.

PREPARATION TIME: 20 minutes, plus chilling
COOKING TIME: 15 minutes   **SERVES:** 4

200 g (7 oz) butter
1 small head fennel, finely chopped
1 teaspoon finely grated lemon rind
1 teaspoon fennel seeds, crushed
4 small round pitta breads
350 g (11½ oz) raw peeled prawns
1 garlic clove, crushed
good pinch of paprika
¼ teaspoon ground mace
salt and pepper

1 Melt 15 g (½ oz) of the butter in a frying pan and fry the fennel gently for 5 minutes or until soft. Stir in the lemon rind, fennel seeds and seasoning. Split the pittas down one side and spread the fennel mixture inside. Flatten them firmly under the palms of your hands.

2 Melt another 25 g (1 oz) of the butter in a large frying pan and gently fry the prawns for about 2 minutes, turning once, or until they are deep pink on both sides. (Fry in batches if necessary.) Return all the prawns to the pan and stir in the garlic, paprika and mace.

3 Pack the prawns into 4 individual 125 ml (4 fl oz) ramekin dishes. Melt the remaining butter in a small saucepan, skimming off any foam from the surface. Spoon over the prawns so that they are mostly submerged. Cover and chill for 2 hours or until the butter has set.

4 Heat a ridged grill pan or grill and lightly toast the pittas on both sides. Cut into fingers and serve with the prawns.

Potted prawns with fennel pittas

The best prawn cocktail

This is a far better prawn cocktail than the one you will be served in most restaurants. It's made with freshly cooked prawns, and the mayonnaise has a fresh tang of lime juice and ginger. Use homemade mayonnaise (see page 20) or a good-quality bought one.

PREPARATION TIME: 15 minutes

COOKING TIME: 3–5 minutes **SERVES:** 4

2 tablespoons olive oil

300 g (10 oz) raw peeled prawns

15 g (½ oz) fresh root ginger

150 ml (¼ pint) Mayonnaise (see page 20) or good-quality shop-bought mayonnaise

3 tablespoons natural yogurt

1 tablespoon sun-dried tomato paste

1 teaspoon caster sugar

1 tablespoon lime juice

½ romaine or cos lettuce

plenty of basil leaves

salt and pepper

lime wedges, to serve

1 Heat the oil in a large frying pan. Add the prawns and fry for 1–2 minutes on each side until they are deep pink. Sprinkle with a little seasoning and drain to a plate to cool.

2 Peel and finely grate the ginger, working over a plate to catch the juice. Mix the ginger and juice in a bowl with the mayonnaise, yogurt, tomato paste, sugar, lime juice and a little seasoning. Beat well.

3 Tear the lettuce leaves into small serving bowls and add plenty of basil leaves to each bowl. Pile the cooled prawns on top. Spoon over the sauce and serve with lime wedges.

Garlic prawn tapas
These spice-coated prawns taste so good that they are worthy of a main meal, served with plenty of tasty bread and other little nibbles. If you're entertaining, prepare everything in advance and put it in the refrigerator, well covered, until you're ready to cook.

PREPARATION TIME: 10 minutes

COOKING TIME: 10 minutes   **SERVES:** 4

2 garlic cloves, crushed

1 teaspoon paprika

1 medium-hot red chilli, deseeded and
   finely chopped

2 tablespoons extra virgin olive oil

500 g (1 lb) large whole raw prawns

salt

Aïoli (see page 20), to serve

1 Mix together the garlic, paprika, chilli, oil and a little salt in a large bowl. (If you're preparing this in advance, leave the salt until you're ready to cook.)

2 Add the prawns and toss them in the mixture until they are evenly coated.

3 Heat a ridged grill pan or heavy-based frying pan and add half the prawns, spreading them in a single layer. Cook for 2–3 minutes or until they are deep pink on the underside. Turn and cook for a further 1–2 minutes. Transfer to a warm dish and cook the remainder in the same way. Serve with the Aïoli.

Lobster tails with chilli mojito

Lobster is such a treat that it's worth dressing it up with an equally indulgent sauce. If you're not used to cooking lobster, the tails are worth buying because they need minimal preparation and there's little waste. This recipe serves two, but quantities can easily be doubled for a larger group.

PREPARATION TIME: 10 minutes, plus marinating

COOKING TIME: 8–10 minutes　　**SERVES:** 2

2 raw lobster tails

finely grated rind and juice of 1 lime

2 teaspoons caster sugar

several sprigs of mint, roughly chopped

¼ teaspoon crushed dried chillies

1 tablespoon white rum

1 tablespoon mild olive oil

salt and pepper

watercress, to serve

1 Use a pair of scissors to cut away the flat sides of the lobster tails and the fins to expose the flesh. Push a wooden skewer through the length of each tail to keep them flat and stop them curling up as they cook. Place the tails, flesh sides up, in a shallow dish.

2 Put the lime rind and juice, sugar, mint and dried chilli in a small bowl and pound with the end of a rolling pin to bruise the mint and mingle the flavours. Add the rum and a little seasoning.

3 Spoon the dressing over the lobster flesh. (At this stage, you can cover and chill the lobster for several hours until you are ready to cook.)

4 Drizzle with the oil and cook under a preheated grill for 8–10 minutes or until the shells are red and the flesh has turned pink. Serve hot on a bed of watercress.

Tip This recipe works equally well on the barbecue. Cook over the coals, turning frequently, until cooked as above.

Crayfish with spicy coriander salsa

Crayfish are miniature freshwater lobster. They can be difficult to buy and, like lobster, make a rare treat. Cooked Dublin Bay prawns (also known as langoustines) or even ordinary large prawns are a useful substitute.

PREPARATION TIME: 15 minutes

COOKING TIME: 6–7 minutes   **SERVES:** 2

2 tomatoes, skinned

2 tablespoons mild olive oil

1 teaspoon cumin seeds, lightly crushed

1 teaspoon coriander seeds, lightly crushed

2 garlic cloves, finely chopped

1 teaspoon chopped lemon thyme

12 whole raw crayfish

1 small avocado, peeled, stoned and finely chopped

salt and pepper

1 Halve the tomatoes and discard the seeds. Finely dice the flesh. Heat 1 tablespoon of the oil in a frying pan and gently fry the cumin and coriander seeds for 1 minute. Add the garlic and lemon thyme and cook for a further minute. Remove from the heat and leave to cool.

2 Bring a large saucepan of salted water to the boil and drop in the crayfish, one at a time. Cook for 4–5 minutes or until they float to the surface. Drain well.

3 Spread the crayfish flat on the chopping board and cut off the heads. Halve the tails lengthways and arrange them on a serving platter.

4 Beat the spice and herb mixture in a bowl with the diced tomatoes and avocado. Season to taste and spoon over the crayfish to serve.

Devilled oysters

This is a good recipe to try if you baulk at the idea of eating raw oysters. When you buy them, try and get an oyster knife, which makes the task of shucking the oysters much easier.

PREPARATION TIME: 25 minutes

COOKING TIME: 15 minutes   **SERVES:** 4

12 oysters

1 teaspoon mustard seeds

75 g (3 oz) butter

2 shallots, finely chopped

½ celery stick, finely chopped

1 garlic clove, crushed

1 tablespoon white wine vinegar

1 teaspoon Tabasco sauce

1 tablespoon chopped chives

1 tablespoon chopped flat leaf parsley

plenty of sea or rock salt and pepper

1 To shuck the oysters, hold an oyster, wrapped in a heavy-weight cloth, with the rounded shell underneath. Push a strong knife, preferably an oyster knife, into the small gap at the hinged end. Twist the knife to sever the muscle and separate the shells.

2 Discard the top shell. Run the blade of the knife under the oyster to loosen it, holding the shell steady to prevent the juices from running out. Place the oyster in a grill pan, lined with a layer of salt to keep the shells from flopping over, and repeat with the remainder.

3 Dry-fry the mustard seeds in a frying pan until they start to pop. Add the butter, the shallots and celery and fry for 3 minutes. Add the garlic and a little seasoning and fry for a further 2 minutes. Stir in the vinegar, Tabasco sauce and two-thirds of each herb.

4 Spoon the mixture over the oysters and cook under a preheated grill for 5–8 minutes or until the oysters are just firm. Serve scattered with the remaining herbs.

Devilled oysters

Tea-smoked clams

You will need smallish clams, about 5 cm (2 inches) across, for this recipe. Avoid ones that are too large because they'll be too chewy, while the very tiny ones are best used in sauces. You can cook the clams in advance so that they're ready for smoking just before you serve them.

PREPARATION TIME: 25 minutes

COOKING TIME: 20 minutes **SERVES:** 4

50 ml (2 fl oz) white wine

2 garlic cloves, crushed

1 kg (2 lb) clams, cleaned (see page 12)

4 tablespoons strong tealeaves (such as jasmine)

4 tablespoons long-grain rice

75 ml (3 fl oz) red wine vinegar

50 ml (2 fl oz) groundnut oil or mild olive oil

1 tablespoon sesame oil

1 medium-strength red chilli, deseeded and finely
  sliced

1 tablespoon clear honey

3 tablespoons chopped chives

salt and pepper

1 Bring the wine and garlic to the boil in a large saucepan. Tip in the clams, cover with a tight-fitting lid and cook for 4–5 minutes or until the shells have opened. Drain and discard any clams that remain closed.

2 Line a large, heavy-based frying pan with foil and scatter in the tealeaves and rice. Position a small rack over the top (a small wire cooling rack is ideal). Heat the pan until the tea mixture starts to smoke.

3 Reduce the heat and scatter the clams on to the rack. Cover with a tent of foil and cook over the lowest heat for 15 minutes.

4 Meanwhile, mix together the vinegar, oils, chilli, honey, chives and seasoning. Transfer the clams to warm serving bowls and spoon over the dressing. Serve warm.

Mussel gratin

Smothered in garlic, herbs and a crispy crumb topping, these little treats make a delicious nibble to serve with drinks. Alternatively, serve them as a starter, arranged on a bed of herb salad. Ideally, use fairly large mussels, so that they're not too fiddly to prepare.

PREPARATION TIME: 20 minutes

COOKING TIME: 10 minutes   **SERVES:** 4

4 tablespoons white wine

500 g (1 lb) mussels, cleaned (see page 12)

75 g (3 oz) crème fraîche

50 g (2 oz) butter

2 garlic cloves, crushed

75 g (3 oz) breadcrumbs

4 tablespoons finely chopped mixed herbs (such as
   tarragon, parsley, dill and thyme)

salt and pepper

1 Put the wine in a large saucepan and heat until bubbling. Tip in the mussels, cover with a tight-fitting lid and cook for 4–5 minutes or until opened. Drain, reserving the cooking juices, and leave to cool slightly. Discard any shells that remain closed.

2 Remove the mussels from their shells. Break the shells apart and arrange half the shells (choose the largest) in a single layer on a foil-lined grill rack. Place a mussel in each.

3 Blend the crème fraîche with 4 tablespoons of the mussel cooking juices and spoon into the shells.

4 Melt the butter in a frying pan and stir in the garlic, breadcrumbs, herbs and a little seasoning. Spoon the mixture over the mussels and cook under a preheated moderate grill until lightly toasted.

Scallops with asparagus and frazzled bacon

Sautéeing scallops in bacon juices and serving with asparagus is such a simple treat for this very special shellfish.

PREPARATION TIME: 15 minutes

COOKING TIME: 25 minutes   **SERVES:** 4

½ **small leek**

300 g (10 oz) **asparagus**

50 g (2 oz) **butter**

2 tablespoons **single cream**

75 g (3 oz) **thin-cut rashers of smoked streaky bacon**

12 **plump shelled scallops (see page 13)**

salt and pepper

4 tablespoons **chopped chervil or parsley, to serve**

1 Trim and slice the leek. Discard the tough stalk ends from the asparagus and cut the stems into 5 cm (2 inch) lengths. Melt 15 g (½ oz) of the butter in a frying pan and gently fry the leek for about 5 minutes or until it is softened. Add the asparagus, cover with a lid and cook on the lowest heat for 6–7 minutes or until just tender.

2 Tip the mixture into a food processor and blend to a smooth purée. Blend in the cream and transfer the purée to a small saucepan.

3 Halve the bacon rashers lengthways and then widthways to make short strips and cook in a clean frying pan until crisp and golden. Drain and keep warm.

4 Heat the asparagus purée through gently while you cook the scallops. Add the scallops to the very hot frying pan, sprinkle with a little seasoning and cook for 2–3 minutes on each side.

5 Spoon the purée on to serving plates and arrange the scallops with the bacon on top. Melt the remaining butter in the pan and drizzle over the scallops. Serve sprinkled with chervil or parsley.

Scallops with asparagus and frazzled bacon

Feta-stuffed squid

This makes a brilliant barbecue dish when you're looking for something a bit different, but it also works well in a ridged grill pan. Once stuffed, the skewered squid will keep in the refrigerator overnight, but make sure it's tightly wrapped.

PREPARATION TIME: 25 minutes, plus cooling
COOKING TIME: 15–20 minutes   **SERVES:** 6

40 g (1½ oz) bulgar wheat
2 garlic cloves, roughly chopped
2 spring onions, roughly sliced
several sprigs each of mint and parsley
finely grated rind of 1 lemon
4 tablespoons olive oil
200 g (7 oz) feta cheese
12 squid tubes, each 10–12 cm (4–5 inches) long,
   cleaned (see page 13)
salt and pepper

1 Put the bulgar wheat in a saucepan and cover with plenty of boiling water. Cook for 8–10 minutes or until only just tender. Drain through a sieve and leave to cool.

2 Put the garlic, spring onions, herbs, lemon rind and a little seasoning in a food processor and blend briefly until finely chopped. Add 2 tablespoons of the oil and the bulgar wheat and crumble in the feta. Blend briefly until the mixture forms a crumbly paste but is not too finely minced.

3 Use a small teaspoon to pack the mixture into the squid tubes. Push each filled piece of squid on to a skewer by threading the skewer through the thin end of the squid and then back through both sides of the wide end to secure the filling. Brush with the remaining oil and a little pepper.

4 Cook on the barbecue or in a preheated ridged grill pan for 5–10 minutes, turning once, until the squid is beginning to colour. Serve hot.

Salt and pepper squid

You will need medium-sized squid tubes, 10–12 cm (4–5 inches) long, for this recipe. If you use very small tubes, they'll curl up into rings, but the very large ones will be too coarse.

PREPARATION TIME: 15 minutes

COOKING TIME: 6–8 minutes   **SERVES:** 4

500 g (1 lb) medium-sized squid, cleaned (see page 13)

½ teaspoon Sichuan peppercorns, crushed

¼ teaspoon black peppercorns, crushed

½ teaspoon sea salt

4 tablespoons sunflower oil

1 medium-strength red chilli, deseeded and thinly sliced

Salad:

½ cucumber, peeled

50 g (2 oz) watercress

2 spring onions, shredded

2 tablespoons dark soy sauce

2 tablespoons sesame oil

2 teaspoons caster sugar

1 Make the salad. Cut the cucumber into long, fine strips and toss with the watercress and spring onions. Mix the soy sauce in a small bowl with the sesame oil and sugar.

2 Halve each squid lengthways so that you end up with 2 flat triangles. Using the tip of a small, sharp knife, score the inner side of each piece, making sure you don't cut right through. Pat the pieces dry on kitchen paper. Mix together the peppers and sea salt.

3 Heat 2 tablespoons of the oil in a large frying pan or wok and fry the chilli for 15–30 seconds until it begins to colour. Drain with a slotted spoon. Add half the squid and fry for 2–3 minutes or until it starts to colour. Drain with a slotted spoon and fry the remainder in the remaining oil.

4 Return all the squid to the pan and sprinkle with the salt and pepper mixture, stir-frying until evenly coated. Transfer to serving plates and scatter with the fried chilli. Spoon a little salad beside each portion of the squid and drizzle with the dressing.

Broad bean and anchovy tapas

This is pretty much a storecupboard dish – a simple blend of ingredients that tastes fabulous. Serve as a tapas-style starter with warm bread to mop up the oil, a bowl of olives and some salted almonds.

PREPARATION TIME: 15 minutes

COOKING TIME: 10 minutes   **SERVES:** 4–6

350 g (11½ oz) shelled broad beans

2 x 50 g (2 oz) cans anchovy fillets in olive oil

5 tablespoons extra virgin olive oil

1 small red onion, finely chopped

2 garlic cloves, crushed

1 teaspoon finely chopped rosemary

pepper

1 Cook the beans in a saucepan of boiling water for about 5 minutes or until tender. Drain and rinse in cold water. Pop the beans out of their shells and put them in a bowl.

2 Drain the anchovies, reserving the oil, and cut the fillets into diagonal slices, about 1 cm (½ inch) wide.

3 Heat 1 tablespoon of the extra virgin olive oil in a frying pan and gently fry the onion for 5 minutes or until softened. Stir in the garlic and rosemary and fry for 1 minute.

4 Add the sliced anchovies, their oil and the remaining extra virgin olive oil. Tip into the bowl of beans and toss the ingredients together, seasoning to taste with a little pepper. Cover and chill until ready to serve.

Pissaladière

Use fresh anchovies or whitebait to top this buttery onion tart. The pastry is so quick and easy, yet tastes great. Just remember to make it in advance so that you can chill it before rolling.

PREPARATION TIME: 30 minutes, plus chilling
COOKING TIME: 45 minutes   **SERVES:** 6

225 g (7½ oz) plain flour
175 g (6 oz) lightly salted butter, cut into small dice
1 teaspoon lemon juice
5 tablespoons olive oil
500 g (1 lb) onions, thinly sliced
1 tablespoon chopped lemon thyme
200 g (7 oz) fresh anchovy fillets or whitebait
handful of black olives
pepper
chopped parsley, to serve

1 Put the flour in a bowl and add the butter. Mix the lemon juice with 100 ml (3½ fl oz) ice-cold water and add it to the bowl. Mix with a round-bladed knife until the dough clings together.

2 Turn out the dough on to a floured surface and roll it out to 30 × 10 cm (12 × 4 inches). Fold the bottom third up and the upper third down to make a square of 3 layers. Give the pastry a quarter turn. Repeat the rolling, folding and turning 4 more times, then wrap and chill for 30 minutes.

3 Heat 3 tablespoons of the oil in a saucepan and add the onions. Fry gently for about 20 minutes, stirring frequently, until deep golden, adding the thyme for the last few minutes.

4 Thinly roll out the pastry on a lightly floured surface and cut out 6 squares, each 10 × 10 cm (4 × 4 inches). Transfer to a lightly greased baking sheet and pinch up the edges of the pastry to make cases. Scatter with the fried onions, spreading them almost to the edges.

5 Scatter with the fish and olives and drizzle with the remaining oil and a little black pepper. Bake in a preheated oven, 220°C (425°F), Gas Mark 7, for 20–25 minutes or until the pastry is golden. Sprinkle with parsley and serve either warm or cold.

Red mullet tartlets with sauce vierge
The combination of red mullet, tomatoes and colourful, herby sauce is really stunning in these little pastries.

PREPARATION TIME: 25 minutes

COOKING TIME: 30 minutes   **SERVES:** 6

8 red mullet fillets

100 ml (3½ fl oz) extra virgin olive oil

1 teaspoon coriander seeds, crushed

15 g (½ oz) fresh herbs (such as parsley, basil and chives), finely chopped

2 garlic cloves, crushed

finely grated rind and juice of 1 lemon

400 g (13 oz) puff pastry (thawed if frozen)

1 egg yolk, to glaze

350 g (11½ oz) cherry tomatoes, halved

salt and pepper

1 Season the red mullet fillets. Heat 2 tablespoons of the oil in a large frying pan and fry the fillets briefly on both sides. Slice the fish into chunky pieces.

2 In a small bowl, whisk together the coriander seeds, herbs, garlic, lemon rind and juice, the remaining olive oil and a little seasoning. Pour the mixture into a small saucepan, ready to reheat.

3 Roll out the pastry on a lightly floured surface and cut out 6 rounds, each 12 cm (5 inches) across, using a cutter or small bowl as a guide. Place them on a lightly greased baking sheet and use the tip of a sharp knife to make a shallow cut 1 cm (½ inch) from the edge of each round. Brush the rims with egg yolk. Bake in a preheated oven, 220°C (425°F), Gas Mark 7, for 15 minutes or until well risen and golden. Scoop out the risen centres of the pastries.

4 Pile the tomatoes and fish into the tartlets and return to the oven for a further 10 minutes. Meanwhile, reheat the sauce. Transfer the tartlets to serving plates and spoon some sauce over each.

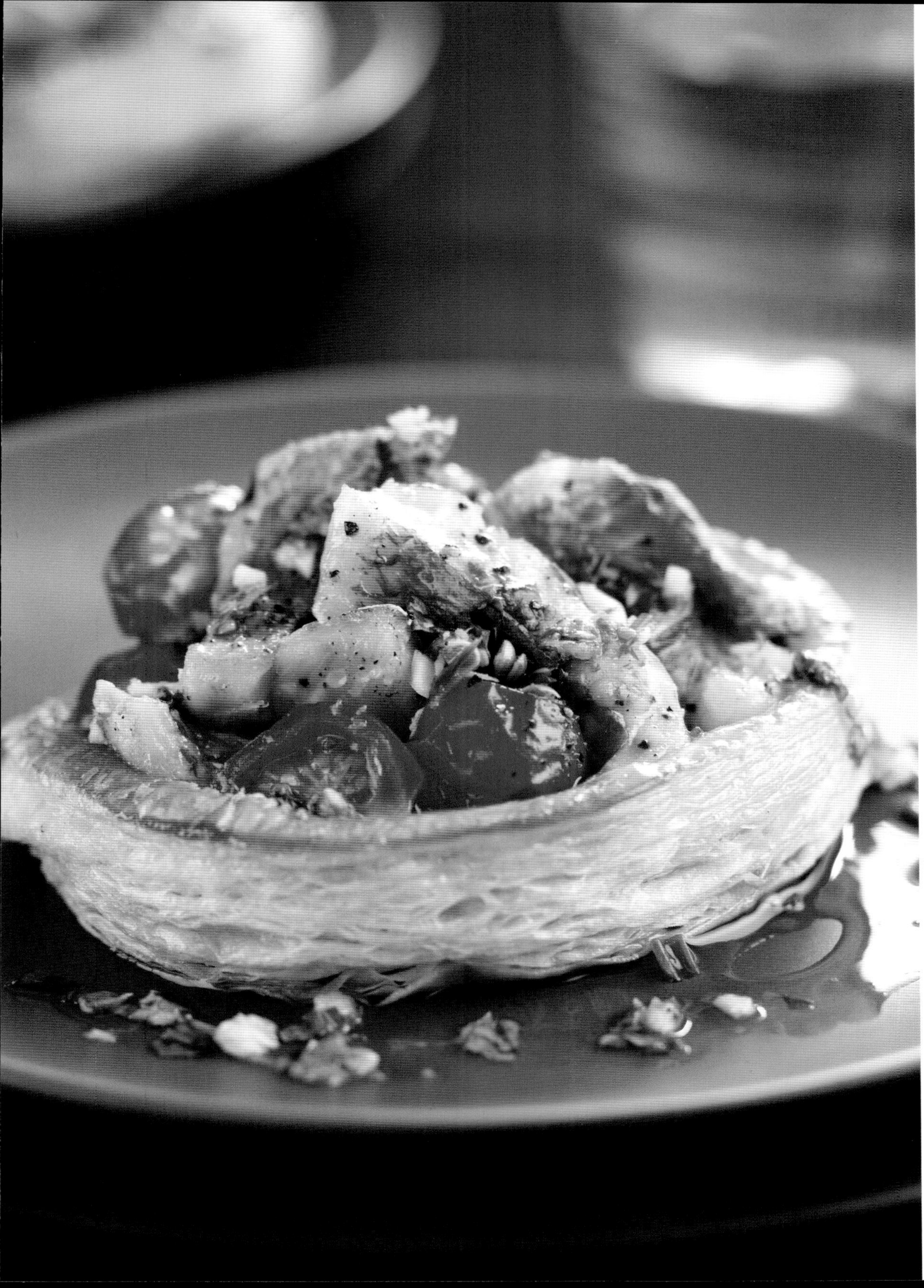

Red mullet tartlets with sauce vierge

Mackerel and wild rice niçoise

Fresh mackerel makes a far more interesting alternative to the more regularly used canned tuna in this colourful salad. Alternatively, use fresh tuna steaks, frying them in a little olive oil for two to three minutes on each side so that they're just pink in the centre.

PREPARATION TIME: 20 minutes

COOKING TIME: 25 minutes   SERVES: 3–4

100 g (3½ oz) wild rice

150 g (5 oz) French beans, halved

300 g (10 oz) large mackerel fillets

6 tablespoons olive oil

12 black olives

8 canned anchovy fillets in olive oil, drained and
    halved

250 g (8 oz) cherry tomatoes, halved

3 hard-boiled eggs, cut into quarters

1 tablespoon lemon juice

1 tablespoon French mustard

2 tablespoons chopped chives

salt and pepper

1 Cook the rice in plenty of boiling water for 20–25 minutes or until it is tender. (The grains will start to split open when they're just cooked.) Add the French beans and cook for 2 minutes.

2 Meanwhile, lay the mackerel on a foil-lined grill rack and brush with 1 tablespoon of the oil. Grill for 8–10 minutes or until cooked through. Leave to cool.

3 Drain the rice and beans and mix together in a salad bowl with the olives, anchovies, tomatoes and eggs. Flake the mackerel, discarding any stray bones, and add to the bowl.

4 Mix the remaining oil with the lemon juice, mustard, chives and a little seasoning and add to the bowl. Toss the ingredients lightly together, cover and chill until ready to serve.

Sardine salad with herb and caper dressing
As lovely as plain grilled or barbecued sardines are, it's good to be experimental with them now and again. This fresh, clean-tasting salad makes an appetizing summer starter – preferably eaten outdoors! – or a light meal for two.

PREPARATION TIME: 20 minutes

COOKING TIME: 50 minutes   **SERVES:** 4

400 g (13 oz) young raw beetroot

6 tablespoons extra virgin olive oil

500 g (1 lb) sardines, gutted, with heads and tails removed

1 small garlic clove, finely chopped

1 tablespoon lemon juice

1 teaspoon finely chopped rosemary

2 tablespoons capers, rinsed and drained

50 g (2 oz) rocket or herb salad

125 g (4 oz) mild goats' cheese

salt and pepper

1 Trim and scrub the beetroot, then cut into small wedges. Put the pieces in a small roasting tin and toss with 1 tablespoon of the oil. Roast in a preheated oven, 200°C (400°F), Gas Mark 6, for 40 minutes or until just tender. Add the sardines to the tin and drizzle with another 1 tablespoon of the oil. Roast for a further 10 minutes or until the sardines are cooked through.

2 Whisk together the remaining oil, garlic, lemon juice, rosemary, capers and salt and pepper to taste.

3 Cut the sardines along the backbones and lift the fillets from the bones.

4 Put the salad leaves on serving plates and arrange the beetroot and sardines on top. Crumble or chop the goats' cheese. Scatter it over the top and spoon over the dressing.

Tuna polpettes

Made using either minced meat or fish, polpettes are a Mediterranean version of a burger. This recipe uses fresh tuna, but can be made equally well with swordfish or shark.

PREPARATION TIME: 20 minutes

COOKING TIME: 35 minutes   **SERVES:** 4

25 g (1 oz) bread

2 tablespoons milk

1 small red onion, finely chopped

3 tablespoons olive oil

500 g (1 lb) fresh tuna, cut into chunks

Roasted Tomato Sauce (see page 21)

150 g (5 oz) mozzarella cheese

1 tablespoon finely chopped oregano

salt and pepper

1 Break the bread into pieces and soak them in a bowl with the milk until soft. Mash to a pulp. Fry the onion in 1 tablespoon of the oil in a frying pan for about 5 minutes or until softened. Push the tuna through a mincer or briefly use a food processor to mince the fish, taking care not to mince it to a purée.

2 Mix together the tuna, onion, bread and a little seasoning. Divide the mixture into 8 equal portions. Roll each into a ball and flatten into little burger shapes.

3 Heat the remaining oil in the frying pan and fry the polpettes on both sides to brown. Tip half the tomato sauce into a shallow, ovenproof dish and arrange the polpettes over the sauce.

4 Cut the mozzarella into 8 thin slices and arrange them over the polpettes. Scatter with the oregano and seasoning and bake in a preheated oven, 180°C (350°F), Gas Mark 4, for 20–25 minutes or until heated through. Meanwhile, reheat the remaining sauce to serve.

Tuna polpettes

Sushi

This simplified version of rolled sushi is very similar in flavour but takes half the time to make. You can use any mixture of fish as long as you can be sure that it's absolutely fresh.

PREPARATION TIME: 30 minutes, plus cooling

COOKING TIME: 15 minutes   **SERVES:** 4–6

225 g (7½ oz) Japanese sushi rice

4 spring onions, very finely shredded

4 tablespoons seasoned rice vinegar

1 tablespoon caster sugar

25 g (1 oz) pickled ginger, shredded

1 tablespoon toasted sesame seeds

100 g (3½ oz) wild salmon

1 large sole fillet

3–4 sheets nori

10 peeled cooked prawns

light soy sauce, to serve

1 Put the rice in a heavy-based saucepan with 450 ml (¾ pint) water. Bring slowly to the boil, then reduce the heat and simmer, half-covered with a lid, for 5–8 minutes or until all the water is absorbed. Cover completely and cook very gently for 5 minutes or until the rice is very tender and sticky. Turn into a bowl and leave to cool.

2 Stir the spring onions, vinegar, sugar, ginger and sesame seeds into the rice. Slice the salmon and sole into small strips.

3 Use scissors to cut the nori sheets into 6 cm (2½ inch) squares. Dampen your hands and mould the rice into little ovals. Arrange the rice ovals diagonally over the nori squares.

4 Bring the pointed ends on opposite sides of the nori over the rice and arrange a piece of fish or a prawn on top. Arrange on a serving platter and serve with a small bowl of soy sauce for dipping.

Sushi

Main courses

There are so many delicious ways to cook fish for a main course that it's impossible to contain them all in one chapter. The following pages include a selection of the best from the classics to the more innovative ideas. Whether you prefer simply to grill or pan-fry delicious fillets, or want to try something more complicated, such as wrapping succulent portions in greaseproof paper, remember that many recipes can be adapted to suit the fish that is available. Unlike many meat dishes, fish recipes are almost endlessly flexible.

Sea bream in a salt crust

This Spanish cooking technique is one of the best ways to enjoy absolutely fresh fish. It traps all the flavour and succulence and, amazingly, is not overly salty to taste.

PREPARATION TIME: 15 minutes

COOKING TIME: 25 minutes **SERVES:** 4

1.75 kg (3½ lb) coarse sea salt

1.25–1.5 kg (2½–3 lb) sea bream

small bunch of herbs (such as thyme, parsley and fennel)

1 lemon, sliced

pepper

Aïoli (see page 20), lemon wedges and extra herbs, to serve

1 Use foil to line a roasting tin that is large enough to hold the whole fish and scatter the base with a thin layer of salt. Rinse the fish but do not dry it and place it on top of the salt, diagonally if necessary. Tuck the herbs and lemon slices into the cavity and season with black pepper.

2 Pull up the foil around the fish so that there is a lining of salt about 1.5 cm (¾ inch) thick around the fish.

3 Scatter the fish with an even covering of salt about 1 cm (½ inch) thick. Drizzle or spray the salt with a little water and bake in a preheated oven, 200°C (400°F), Gas Mark 6, for 25 minutes. To check that the fish is cooked, pierce a metal skewer into the thickest area of the fish and leave for a few seconds before removing. If the skewer is very hot, the fish is cooked through.

4 Lift away the salt crust and peel away the skin. Serve the fish in chunky pieces and then lift away the central bone and head so that you can serve the bottom fillet. Serve with lemon wedges, Aïoli and herbs.

Tip Several whole white fish can be served in this way. Sea bass or snapper are really good or, if you can get one, a small turbot.

Sea bream in a salt crust

Braised cod with lentils
A bed of garlicky lentils and tomatoes gives the fish plenty of colour and flavour contrast. Serve with baby boiled potatoes or chunks of bread for mopping up the juices. See page 16 for some alternatives to cod.

PREPARATION TIME: 15 minutes

COOKING TIME: 40 minutes   **SERVES:** 4

150 g (5 oz) Puy lentils

3 tablespoons extra virgin olive oil

1 large onion, finely chopped

3 garlic cloves, sliced

several sprigs of rosemary or thyme

200 ml (7 fl oz) Fish Stock (see page 17)

4 chunky pieces cod fillet, skinned

8 small tomatoes

salt and pepper

2 tablespoons chopped flat leaf parsley, to serve

1 Boil the lentils in plenty of water for 15 minutes. Drain.

2 Meanwhile, heat 1 tablespoon of the oil in a frying pan and fry the onion for 5 minutes. Stir in the garlic and fry for a further 2 minutes.

3 Add the lentils, rosemary or thyme, stock and a little seasoning to the frying pan and bring to the boil.

4 Pour into a shallow, ovenproof dish and arrange the cod on top. Score the tops of the tomatoes and tuck them around the fish. Drizzle with the remaining oil.

5 Bake, uncovered, in a preheated oven, 180°C (350°F), Gas Mark 4, for 25 minutes or until the fish is cooked through. Serve sprinkled with parsley.

Pan-fried sea bass with lemon and caper butter *If only small whole sea bass are available, choose chunky halibut, monkfish or hake fillets instead.*

PREPARATION TIME: 20 minutes

COOKING TIME: 25 minutes   SERVES: 4

875 g (1¾ lb) large potatoes

4 sea bass fillets, each about 200 g (7 oz)

1 lemon

100 g (3½ oz) butter

2 tablespoons olive oil

2 tablespoons capers, rinsed and drained

6 tablespoons chopped mixed herbs (such as parsley, tarragon, dill and chervil)

pepper

1 Cut the potatoes into large chunks and cook them in plenty of boiling, lightly salted water until tender. Meanwhile, check over the fish fillets for any bones and pat them dry on kitchen paper. Season lightly on all sides. Use a zester to pare the rind from the lemon and squeeze the juice.

2 While the potatoes are cooking, melt 15 g (½ oz) of the butter in a large frying pan with the oil. Add the fish fillets, skin side down (if unskinned), and fry gently for 5 minutes or until the skin starts to colour. Turn the fillets over and fry for a further 5 minutes or until cooked through. Drain and keep warm.

3 Drain the potatoes and lightly crush them in the colander so that they are broken into small pieces but not completely mashed. Melt another 25 g (1 oz) of the butter in the potato pan. Return the potatoes to the pan with plenty of pepper and stir together to mix.

4 Melt the remaining butter in the frying pan, add the capers, herbs and lemon juice and heat through, stirring, until the butter has melted.

5 Pile the potatoes on to serving plates, arrange the fish fillets on top and spoon over the herb sauce. Scatter with the lemon rind.

Fish and chips

Homemade fish and chips tends to be lighter and less greasy than bought ones and are not much bother to make. Have everything ready for last-minute cooking for a speedy supper.

PREPARATION TIME: 25 minutes

COOKING TIME: 30 minutes   **SERVES:** 4

125 g (4 oz) self-raising flour, plus a little extra for dusting
½ teaspoon baking powder
¼ teaspoon ground turmeric
1.5 kg (3 lb) large potatoes
750 g (1½ lb) piece skinned cod or haddock fillet
sunflower oil or groundnut oil, for deep-frying
salt and pepper
Crushed Minted Peas (see page 22), to serve

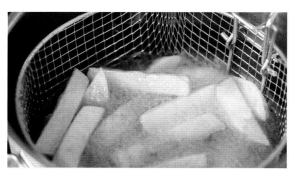

1 Mix together the flour, baking powder, turmeric and a pinch of salt and make a well in the centre. Measure 200 ml (7 fl oz) cold water and add half to the well. Gradually whisk the liquid into the flour to make a smooth batter. Whisk in the remainder.

2 Cut the potatoes into 1.5 cm (¾ inch) slices, then cut across to make chunky chips. Put them in a bowl of cold water.

3 Check the fish for any stray bones, pat dry on kitchen paper and cut into 4 portions. Season lightly and dust with extra flour. Thoroughly drain the chips and pat them dry on kitchen paper.

4 Pour the oil into a deep-fat fryer or large, sturdy saucepan until it is one-third full. Heat the oil to 180–190°C (350–375°F) or until a spoonful of batter turns golden in 30 seconds. Fry half the chips for 10 minutes or until golden. Drain and keep warm while you cook the remainder.

5 Dip 2 fish pieces in the batter and lower them into the hot oil. Fry gently for 4–5 minutes or until crisp and golden. Drain and keep warm while you fry the other pieces. Serve with the peas.

Grilled hake with tapenade

Hake is a member of the cod family and has a similarly delicious flavour and texture. The two are also completely interchangeable in recipes. This recipe gives hake a Mediterranean flavour – it is simply grilled and topped with homemade tapenade.

PREPARATION TIME: 15 minutes

COOKING TIME: 10 minutes   **SERVES:** 4

75 g (3 oz) pitted black olives

1 garlic clove, crushed

4 canned anchovy fillets in olive oil, drained

2 tablespoons capers, rinsed and drained

1 teaspoon chopped oregano

5 tablespoons extra virgin olive oil

4 hake fillets or steaks, each about 200 g (7 oz)

salt and pepper

1 Put the olives in a food processor with the garlic, anchovy fillets, capers, oregano and all but 2 tablespoons of the oil.

2 Blend to a thick paste, scraping the mixture down from the side of the bowl if necessary. Season the tapenade with pepper and transfer to a small bowl. Cover and set aside.

3 Check over the hake fillets or steaks for any stray bones and season with salt and pepper. Lightly oil a foil-lined grill rack. Lay the hake on the foil and drizzle with the remaining oil.

4 Cook under a preheated grill for 8–10 minutes or until cooked through. Transfer to serving plates and top with the tapenade.

Roasted sea bass with fennel

Roasting whole fish over a bed of Mediterranean vegetables is enough to put anyone in a holiday mood. This recipe needs few accompaniments – perhaps simply some chunky oven chips and salad leaves. Turbot is a good alternative to sea bass.

PREPARATION TIME: 20 minutes

COOKING TIME: 25 minutes   **SERVES:** 4

2 heads fennel

2 red onions

1 kg (2 lb) whole sea bass, scaled and gutted

several lemon slices

small bunch of flat leaf parsley

several sprigs of lemon thyme

8–10 black olives

4 canned anchovy fillets in olive oil, drained

5 tablespoons extra virgin olive oil

salt and pepper

1 Thinly slice the fennel and onions and scatter them in a large, shallow, ovenproof dish. Score the fish several times on each side and position it over the vegetables. Tuck the lemon slices and half the herbs into the cavity.

2 Chop the remaining herbs and scatter them into the dish together with the olives and seasoning.

3 Finely chop the anchovy fillets and mash them against the side of a small bowl, gradually blending in the oil.

4 Pour the anchovy oil over the fish and vegetables and bake in a preheated oven, 200°C (400°F), Gas Mark 6, for about 25 minutes or until the fish is cooked through and the vegetables are deep golden and tender.

Variation If you can't get a large fish, use several small ones (one per portion) and arrange them in a single layer over the vegetables in the dish. Reduce the cooking time slightly.

Parchment-baked fish

Sealing portions of fish in their own little parcels is a brilliant way of trapping in all the flavour and moisture. You could try serving mini parcels for starter-sized portions.

PREPARATION TIME: 20 minutes

COOKING TIME: 20 minutes   **SERVES:** 4

2 tablespoons sesame oil, plus extra for brushing

4 shark or swordfish fillets, each about 200 g (7 oz), skinned

75 g (3 oz) shiitake mushrooms, sliced

50 g (2 oz) sugar snap peas, halved lengthways

1 mild red chilli, thinly sliced

40 g (1½ oz) fresh root ginger, grated

2 garlic cloves, crushed

2 tablespoons light soy sauce

2 tablespoons lime juice

2 tablespoons sweet chilli sauce

4 tablespoons chopped fresh coriander

1 Cut out 4 squares, each 30 × 30 cm (12 × 12 inches), of baking parchment and brush the centres of each with a little sesame oil. Place a piece of fish in the centre of each square. Mix together the mushrooms, sugar snap peas and chilli and pile the mixture on top of the fish.

2 Mix together the sesame oil, ginger and garlic and spoon over the vegetables. Bring the sides of the parchment up over the fish as though wrapping a parcel. Fold the edges together and flatten gently.

3 Flatten the ends and fold them over to seal. Place the parcels on a baking sheet and bake in a preheated oven, 190°C (375°F), Gas Mark 5, for 20 minutes. Open one of the parcels and test whether the fish is cooked through. If necessary return to the oven for a few more minutes.

4 Meanwhile, mix together the soy sauce, lime juice, chilli sauce and coriander. Loosen the parcels and spoon the dressing over the fish before serving.

Parchment-baked fish

Roasted monkfish with prosciutto

Firm-fleshed and succulent, thick fillets of monkfish are perfect for roasting with ingredients like garlic and rosemary that you might normally use for a traditional meat roast. Serve with creamy mash and wilted greens.

PREPARATION TIME: 15 minutes

COOKING TIME: 30 minutes   **SERVES:** 5–6

1.5 kg (3 lb) monkfish tail

75 g (3 oz) prosciutto

3 garlic cloves, crushed

2 teaspoons chopped rosemary

1 teaspoon finely grated lemon rind

4 tablespoons olive oil

300 ml (½ pint) white wine

150 ml (¼ pint) crème fraîche

salt and pepper

1 Remove the bone from the monkfish (see page 11) to leave 2 large fillets. Finely chop the prosciutto and mix it with the garlic, rosemary, lemon rind and a little pepper.

2 Spread one of the monkfish fillets with the mixture and place the second fillet on top so that one thick fillet end is against a thin end to make a uniform thickness.

3 Tie the fish at 5 cm (2 inch) intervals with string and place it in a roasting tin. Drizzle with the oil and roast in a preheated oven, 200°C (400°F), Gas Mark 6, for 25 minutes or until the fish is cooked through.

4 Meanwhile, put the wine in a saucepan and cook rapidly over a high heat until reduced by about half.

5 Remove the fish from the oven and transfer it to a serving platter. Remove the string, cover with foil and keep it warm while you make the sauce. Add the reduced wine and crème fraîche to the roasting tin and bring to the boil, stirring until smooth. Season to taste and serve with the fish.

Monkfish and saffron risotto
Monkfish makes such a good choice for a risotto. Firm and meaty in texture, it can be stirred into the creamy rice without breaking up.

PREPARATION TIME: 25 minutes

COOKING TIME: 25 minutes   **SERVES:** 3–4

500 g (1 lb) monkfish, boned (see page 11)

50 g (2 oz) butter

1 onion, chopped

2 garlic cloves, crushed

250 g (8 oz) risotto rice

1 glass dry white wine

1 teaspoon saffron strands

2 teaspoons chopped lemon thyme, plus extra to
   serve

1 litre (1¾ pints) hot Fish Stock (see page 17)

salt and pepper

grated Parmesan cheese, to serve

1 Cut the monkfish into chunks and season lightly. Melt half the butter in a large saucepan and gently fry the onion until it is softened but not browned. Add the fish and cook, stirring, for 2 minutes. Drain the fish and add the garlic to the pan. Cook for 1 minute.

2 Sprinkle in the rice and fry gently for 1 minute. Add the wine and let it bubble until almost evaporated.

3 Add the saffron, thyme and a ladleful of the stock and cook, stirring, until the rice has absorbed the stock. Continue to add the stock, a ladleful at a time, cooking the rice and stirring until the stock is almost absorbed in between each addition.

4 After about 20 minutes, check the consistency of the rice. It should be creamy and tender but slightly firm in the centre. (You might not need all the stock.) Check the seasoning and stir in the fish. Heat through and serve immediately, scattered with Parmesan and chopped thyme.

Fish pie
A good fish pie is a classic, comforting dish that never goes out of fashion. Keep it simple, using just the cod, or dress it up with more luxurious ingredients, such as scallops or prawns.

PREPARATION TIME: 30 minutes

COOKING TIME: 1 hour   **SERVES:** 6

1 kg (2 lb) cod fillet, skinned

3 tablespoons milk

275 g (9 oz) scallops or raw peeled prawns

1.25 kg (2½ lb) floury potatoes

25 g (1 oz) butter

3 large shallots, finely chopped

4 tablespoons chopped tarragon

4 tablespoons chopped parsley

125 g (4 oz) Gruyère cheese, grated

Creamy Béchamel Sauce (see page 18)

salt and pepper

1 Put the cod in a frying pan with the milk and seasoning. Cover and cook gently for 5 minutes. Add the scallops or prawns and cook, covered, for a further 2 minutes. Drain, reserving the liquid, and leave to cool.

2 Bring a saucepan of lightly salted water to the boil. Thinly slice the potatoes and add them to the pan. Return to the boil and cook for 6–8 minutes or until just tender. Drain. Melt the butter in the rinsed-out frying pan and fry the shallots for 5 minutes. Stir in the herbs.

3 Flake the fish into large chunks, discarding any bones, and arrange in a large, shallow, ovenproof dish. Add the scallops or prawns, shallots and herbs.

4 Stir two-thirds of the cheese into the béchamel sauce along with the poaching juices. Pour half over the fish. Layer the potatoes over the top and pour over the remaining sauce. Scatter with the rest of the cheese and bake in a preheated oven, 190°C (375°F), Gas Mark 5, for about 40 minutes or until golden.

Fish pie

Fried snapper with spicy plum sauce

Deep-frying whole fish is an Asian cooking method that adapts well to any firm-fleshed fish, weighing about 400 g (13 oz), which would serve one, or about 625 g (1¼ lb) for two servings. Sea bream or sea bass are particularly good.

PREPARATION TIME: 15 minutes

COOKING TIME: 20 minutes   **SERVES:** 2

625 g (1¼ lb) snapper, scaled and gutted

½ teaspoon Sichuan pepper, crushed

150 ml (¼ pint) groundnut oil or sunflower oil

1 red shallot, finely chopped

1 garlic clove, crushed

25 g (1 oz) fresh root ginger, grated

1 tablespoon light muscovado sugar

500 g (1 lb) red plums, halved and stoned

1 teaspoon Chinese five-spice paste

salt

1 Score diagonal cuts on both sides of the fish. Mix the pepper with a little salt and rub it over the fish, inside and out.

2 Heat 2 tablespoons of the oil in a saucepan. Add the shallot and fry gently for 5 minutes or until softened. Stir in the garlic, ginger, sugar and plums and cover with a lid or foil. Cook gently for 10 minutes or until the plums are pulpy but retain a little texture.

3 Meanwhile, pour the remaining oil into a large frying pan or wok and heat until just smoking. Slide in the fish and cook for 5 minutes, gently moving the fish around by its tail so that it doesn't stick to the base of the pan. Carefully turn the fish and cook for a further 5 minutes or until it is cooked through. Drain to a warm serving plate.

4 Add the five-spice paste to the softened plums and stir gently. The plums should end up softened and slightly pulpy but not puréed. Spoon the plum sauce over the fish and serve.

Skate with balsamic butter and capers

So simple and so full of flavour, this lovely supper dish requires virtually no preparation. It is a good week-night dish, served with new potatoes and a leafy salad.

PREPARATION TIME: 5 minutes

COOKING TIME: 15 minutes   **SERVES:** 2

2 teaspoons plain flour

2 skate wings, each about 200 g (7 oz)

50 g (2 oz) butter

3 tablespoons balsamic vinegar

1 tablespoon capers, rinsed and drained

salt and pepper

1 Mix the flour with a little seasoning and use it to dust the skate.

2 Melt a knob of the butter in a large frying pan and gently fry the skate for about 5 minutes on each side until cooked through. Drain to serving plates and keep warm.

3 Add the remaining butter, balsamic vinegar and capers to the frying pan and cook, whisking until bubbling and syrupy. Check the seasoning and pour over the skate.

Main courses **83**

Brazilian baked snapper
This colourful dish envelops the fish in spicy, aromatic flavours. Some alternatives to snapper, which may not be available, are given on page 16.

PREPARATION TIME: 20 minutes, plus soaking and marinating

COOKING TIME: 1½ hours **SERVES:** 4

250 g (8 oz) black beans

1 kg (2 lb) red snapper, scaled and gutted

juice of 1 lime

3 garlic cloves, chopped

3 bay leaves

2 onions, thinly sliced

4 tablespoons olive oil

several sprigs of parsley

25 g (1 oz) fresh coriander

200 g (7 oz) tomatoes, sliced

1 mild red chilli, deseeded and thinly sliced

salt and pepper

1 Soak the beans overnight in cold water. Season the fish and drizzle inside and out with the lime juice. Chill for 1 hour.

2 Drain the beans, put them in a saucepan with plenty of water and bring to the boil. Boil rapidly for 10 minutes. Drain and return to the pan with the garlic, bay leaves, three-quarters of the sliced onions and 600 ml (1 pint) water. Bring to the boil, reduce the heat and simmer gently, uncovered, for 1½ hours or until tender.

3 Meanwhile, lay the fish in a shallow oiled ovenproof dish. Cover with the parsley and a few coriander sprigs, the tomatoes, chilli and remaining onion. Drizzle with the remaining oil and bake in a preheated oven, 200°C (400°F), Gas Mark 6, for 35 minutes or until cooked through.

4 Drain the fish to a warm plate and tip the contents of the dish into a blender. Add the remaining coriander and blend until smooth. Reheat and season to taste. Serve with the beans and fish.

Brazilian baked snapper

Creamy fish lasagne

Chunky, succulent pieces of fish are a must for this dish so that they're not completely lost between the layers of pasta and sauce. Dried lasagne sheets can be used instead of fresh, but cook them first until they are tender.

PREPARATION TIME: 25 minutes, plus standing

COOKING TIME: 1 hour   **SERVES:** 4–5

2 x 400 g (13 oz) cans chopped tomatoes

1 large onion, finely chopped

2 garlic cloves, crushed

3 tablespoons sun-dried tomato paste

50 g (2 oz) can anchovy fillets in olive oil, drained and chopped

700 g (1 lb 7 oz) skinned haddock fillet,cut into chunks

125 g (4 oz) fresh lasagne sheets

Rich Cheese Sauce (see page 18)

40 g (1½ oz) bread

2 tablespoons olive oil

salt and pepper

1 Put the tomatoes, onion, garlic, tomato paste and a little seasoning in a large saucepan and bring to the boil. Cook for about 10 minutes or until the mixture is thick and pulpy. Stir in half the anchovies and lay the haddock on top. Cook gently for 5 minutes or until the fish is opaque.

2 Spoon one-third of the mixture into a shallow, 1.2 litre (2 pint) ovenproof dish, making sure the pieces of fish are evenly distributed. Arrange a layer of lasagne sheets on top. Cover with half the remaining tomato and fish mixture and spoon over one-third of the cheese sauce. Place another layer of lasagne on top and cover with the remaining tomatoes and fish. Add the remaining lasagne and spoon over the rest of the sauce.

3 Tear the bread into pieces and blend in a food processor to make coarse breadcrumbs. Add the remaining anchovies and blend again until mixed.

4 Scatter over the lasagne and drizzle with the oil. Bake in a preheated oven, 180°C (350°F), Gas Mark 4, for about 45 minutes or until golden. Leave to stand for 10 minutes before serving.

Steamed bream with lemon grass and ginger
This is an incredible healthy, wholesome dish, but one that bursts with lovely fresh flavours. It can be prepared in advance, in its dish, all ready for baking when the time suits you.

PREPARATION TIME: 20 minutes, plus marinating

COOKING TIME: 30 minutes   SERVES: 2

625–750 g (1¼–1½ lb) whole bream, scaled and gutted

1 stalk of lemon grass, trimmed

25 g (1 oz) fresh root ginger, grated

several kaffir lime leaves or Thai basil, torn into pieces

½ bunch of spring onions, chopped

2 garlic cloves, crushed

2 tablespoons light soy sauce

2 tablespoons toasted sesame oil

1 tablespoon clear honey

1 tablespoon cyster sauce

2 tablespoons Chinese cooking wine

4 tablespoons chopped fresh coriander, to serve

1 Score the fish on both sides in a criss-cross pattern and put it on an ovenproof plate or in a shallow baking dish in which it fits quite snugly.

2 Finely slice the lemon grass and mix with the ginger, lime or basil leaves, spring onions, garlic and soy sauce. Pour the marinade over the fish, pushing some into the cavity and the rest over the outside. Cover and chill for 1–2 hours.

3 Scrunch up plenty of foil over the base of a deep roasting tin and press the fish plate or dish on top so that it feels quite secure. Pour boiling water to a depth of 2.5 cm (1 inch) into the tin. Cover the whole tin with a tent of foil. Bake in a preheated oven, 200°C (400°F), Gas Mark 6, for 30 minutes or until the fish is cooked through.

4 Meanwhile, whisk together the sesame oil, honey, oyster sauce and Chinese wine. Carefully lift the plate or dish of cooked fish from the tin. Spoon over the dressing and serve scattered with the chopped coriander.

Chorizo-stuffed plaice with tomatoes

Chorizo sausage makes a fabulous filling for white fish, giving it instant Mediterranean appeal. Any other small flat fish can also be used.

PREPARATION TIME: 20 minutes

COOKING TIME: 25 minutes   **SERVES:** 4

100 g (3½ oz) piece chorizo sausage

50 g (2 oz) breadcrumbs

2 tablespoons sun-dried tomato paste

5 tablespoons olive oil

8 skinned fillets of 2 large plaice

8 small ripe tomatoes or 4 large tomatoes, halved

several sprigs of thyme

splash of white wine

salt and pepper

1 Cut the chorizo into pieces and blend in a food processor until it is finely chopped. Add the breadcrumbs, tomato paste and 1 tablespoon of the oil and blend until combined.

2 Lay the plaice fillets, skinned side up, on the work surface. Spread each with a thin layer of the chorizo mixture and roll up, starting from the thick end.

3 Put the fish in a large, shallow, ovenproof dish and tuck the tomatoes and thyme around the fish. Drizzle with the remaining oil and the wine and season the fish lightly.

4 Bake in a preheated oven, 200°C (400°F), Gas Mark 6, for 20–25 minutes or until cooked through.

Chorizo-stuffed plaice with tomatoes

Roast turbot with saffron and mushroom sauce

Turbot varies enormously in size. A small one might be cooked whole (see Tip below), but larger ones are usually sold as steaks or fillets, which are easier to manage.

PREPARATION TIME: 25 minutes

COOKING TIME: 25 minutes   SERVES: 4

450 ml (¾ pint) Fish Stock (see page 17)

625 g (1¼ lb) turbot fillet or steaks

5 g (¼ oz) tarragon sprigs

½ small leek, thinly sliced

50 g (2 oz) butter, softened

200 g (7 oz) button mushrooms, sliced

½ teaspoon saffron strands

squeeze of lemon juice

100 ml (3½ fl oz) double cream

salt and pepper

1 Put the stock in a saucepan and bring to the boil. Boil until reduced by about two-thirds.

2 Cut the turbot fillet, if using, into 4 equal portions. Season the fish lightly. Scatter half the tarragon sprigs and the leek into a small roasting tin and arrange the turbot on top, skin side up if using fillet. Dot with half the butter and roast in a preheated oven, 200°C (400°F), Gas Mark 6, for 20–25 minutes or until cooked through.

3 Meanwhile, melt the remaining butter in a frying pan and fry the mushrooms until lightly browned. Crumble in the saffron, then pour in the reduced stock, the lemon juice and the cream. Pull the remaining tarragon from the stalks and add to the pan. Bring to the boil and cook until slightly thickened.

4 Transfer the turbot to warm serving plates and strain any cooking juices through a sieve into the mushroom sauce. Spoon the sauce around the fish and serve.

Tip Occasionally, small whole turbot or brill are available from the supermarket or fishmongers. These can be roasted in the same way, over the bed of tarragon and leeks, with the darker skin uppermost. Test that it is cooked through by piercing the thickest area of the flesh with a skewer.

Sole with vermouth butter

Whole grilled lemon sole or Dover sole is such an effortless treat that it's worth keeping its accompaniments equally simple. The flavour of this delicious savoury butter really develops as it melts over the freshly cooked fish.

PREPARATION TIME: 10 minutes, plus cooling

COOKING TIME: 12 minutes **SERVES:** 2

125 ml (4 fl oz) dry vermouth

1 teaspoon fennel seeds, crushed

75 g (3 oz) unsalted butter, softened

1 small garlic clove, crushed

2 tablespoons finely chopped parsley or chervil

2 whole lemon sole or Dover sole

salt and pepper

1 Pour the vermouth into a small saucepan. Bring to the boil and boil until reduced to a scant 1 tablespoon. Pour into a bowl, add the fennel seeds and leave to cool.

2 Add the butter, garlic, parsley or chervil and a little seasoning to the bowl and beat until evenly blended. There will be just enough butter to absorb the reduced vermouth.

3 Lay the fish on a lightly oiled, foil-lined grill rack, dark skin side down, and season lightly. Cook under a preheated grill for 6–8 minutes, turning once, or until cooked through. Transfer to warm serving plates and top with spoonfuls of the butter.

Halibut with sorrel and pancetta

This recipe involves last-minute cooking, but it's simple, so have everything ready and it won't take long. Sorrel can be difficult to find, but spinach makes a good substitute.

PREPARATION TIME: 15 minutes

COOKING TIME: 20 minutes   SERVES: 4

50 g (2 oz) walnuts, roughly chopped

4 halibut fillets, each about 175 g (6 oz), skinned

25 g (1 oz) butter

2 tablespoons walnut oil

1 shallot, finely chopped

50 g (2 oz) pancetta, chopped

200 g (7 oz) sorrel, tough stalks removed

100 g (3½ oz) crème fraîche

salt and pepper

1 Lightly toast the walnuts in a large frying pan and tip them on to a plate. Lightly season the halibut.

2 Melt the butter with the oil in the frying pan and gently fry the shallot and pancetta for about 5 minutes or until golden. Drain with a slotted spoon.

3 Add the halibut fillets to the pan and fry for 2–3 minutes on each side until cooked through. Drain and keep warm. Add the sorrel to the pan and cook very briefly until wilting. Tip on to warm serving plates and top with the fish.

4 Return the shallot and pancetta to the pan and add the crème fraîche. Heat through, season to taste and spoon over the fish.

Crab burgers
This makes four hunky burgers or eight smaller ones and they are great with chunky chips. Serve with Crème Fraîche and Herb Mayonnaise or Roasted Tomato Sauce (see pages 20–21).

PREPARATION TIME: 15 minutes

COOKING TIME: 20–30 minutes   **SERVES:** 4

2 tablespoons olive oil

1 onion, chopped

2 green peppers, deseeded and finely chopped

2 garlic cloves, crushed

½ bunch of spring onions, finely chopped

125 g (4 oz) breadcrumbs

250 g (8 oz) white and brown crabmeat

1 tablespoon Worcestershire sauce

½ teaspoon cayenne pepper

3 tablespoons chopped parsley

1 egg, beaten

sunflower oil, for shallow-frying

salt

iceberg lettuce, to serve

1 Heat the oil in a frying pan and gently fry the onion and green peppers for 5 minutes or until softened. Add the garlic and spring onions and fry for a further 5 minutes. Tip into a bowl.

2 Add the breadcrumbs, crabmeat, Worcestershire sauce, cayenne pepper, parsley and beaten egg and season with a little salt. Mix well with a wooden spoon, or with your hands, until the mixture is evenly combined.

3 Divide the mixture into 4 equal pieces and shape each into a ball. Flatten into a burger shape.

4 Heat a very thin layer of oil in a large frying pan. Fry the burgers (if necessary in 2 batches) for 4–5 minutes on each side until golden. Serve the burgers on a bed of lettuce.

Roasted mackerel with sweet potatoes
Chilli-infused olive oil adds a hot spiciness that's lovely with the cooling mint raita and sweet caramelised potatoes and onions.

PREPARATION TIME: 15 minutes

COOKING TIME: 1 hour **SERVES:** 2

375 g (12 oz) sweet potatoes

1 red onion, thinly sliced

4 tablespoons chilli-infused olive oil

several sprigs of thyme

40 g (1½ oz) sun-dried tomatoes, thinly sliced

4 large mackerel fillets

100 ml (3½ fl oz) natural yogurt

1 tablespoon each of chopped fresh coriander and
  mint

salt and pepper

lemon wedges, to serve

1 Scrub the sweet potatoes and cut them into 1.5 cm (¾ inch) chunks. Scatter the pieces in a shallow, ovenproof dish with the onion. Add the oil, thyme and a little salt and mix together.

2 Bake in a preheated oven, 200°C (400°F), Gas Mark 6, for 40–45 minutes, turning once or twice, until the potatoes are just tender and beginning to brown.

3 Stir in the tomatoes. Fold each mackerel fillet in half, skin side out, and place on top of the potatoes. Return to the oven for a further 12–15 minutes or until the fish is cooked through.

4 Meanwhile, mix together the yogurt, herbs and a little seasoning. Transfer the fish and potatoes to warm serving plates, spoon over the raita and serve with lemon wedges.

Tip Use ready-made chilli oil, or alternatively use mild olive oil instead and add a thinly sliced red chilli when roasting the potatoes.

Herrings with spinach and almond stuffing
Herrings are a good choice for 'dry' methods of cooking because of their natural oiliness. If you don't like dealing with bones, buy herring fillets instead, sandwiching the stuffing between them.

PREPARATION TIME: 25 minutes

COOKING TIME: 35 minutes   **SERVES:** 4

4 boned herrings, heads removed, or 8 fillets

25 g (1 oz) butter, plus extra to grease

4 tablespoons flaked almonds

1 onion, chopped

25 g (1 oz) breadcrumbs

100 g (3½ oz) fresh spinach

plenty of freshly grated nutmeg

25 g (1 oz) Parmesan cheese, grated

salt and pepper

1 Make several slits down each side of the herrings. Melt the butter in a frying pan and fry the almonds until they are beginning to colour. Add the onion and fry gently for 3 minutes.

2 Stir in the breadcrumbs and cook for 1 minute until they start to brown. Scatter the spinach on top, turn off the heat and leave for a couple of minutes or until the spinach has wilted. Season with nutmeg and salt and pepper. Sprinkle with the Parmesan and mix together until evenly combined.

3 Lightly butter a shallow, ovenproof dish. Pack the stuffing into the herring cavities and arrange in the dish. If you are using fillets, arrange 4 fillets in the dish, skin side down, and spread with the stuffing. Press the remaining 4 fillets gently down on top, skin side up.

4 Bake in a preheated oven, 190°C (375°F), Gas Mark 5, for about 25 minutes or until cooked through.

Clams with linguine and tomato pesto

This is an easy-to-make supper dish. The clam and pasta quantities can easily be halved if you're serving two portions.

PREPARATION TIME: 20 minutes

COOKING TIME: 10–20 minutes   **SERVES:** 4

4 tablespoons dry white wine

1 kg (2 lb) small clams, cleaned (see page 12)

300 g (10 oz) fresh linguine or 250 g (8 oz) dried

salt and pepper

Tomato pesto:

150 g (5 oz) sun-dried tomatoes in oil, drained

5 tablespoons pine nuts

8 pitted black olives

2 garlic cloves, roughly sliced

6 tablespoons extra virgin olive oil

40 g (1½ oz) Parmesan cheese, grated, plus extra to
   serve (optional)

2 tomatoes, roughly chopped

1 Make the pesto. Put the sun-dried tomatoes, pine nuts, olives and garlic in a food processor and blend to a thick paste, scraping the mixture down from the side of the bowl.

2 With the machine running, pour in the oil in a steady stream until combined. Add the Parmesan, tomatoes and a little pepper and mix until the tomatoes are finely chopped.

3 Bring the wine to the boil in a large saucepan. Tip in the clams, cover with a tight-fitting lid and cook for 4–5 minutes or until the shells have opened. Drain, reserving the cooking juices and discard any that remain closed. Remove about two-thirds of the clams from their shells.

4 Cook the pasta in plenty of lightly salted boiling water until tender (allow about 2 minutes for fresh pasta and 8–10 minutes for dried). Drain lightly (so there's still plenty of water clinging to the pasta) and return to the pan.

5 Scoop the pesto into the pan with the clams and 4 tablespoons of the clam cooking juices and heat gently for 2 minutes, tossing the ingredients together until mixed. Serve topped with extra Parmesan if liked.

Seafood paella

The secret of a good paella is to sauté the ingredients in the oil before you cook the rice so that the oil carries plenty of flavour. You can substitute other fish and shellfish as you wish.

PREPARATION TIME: 30 minutes

COOKING TIME: 40 minutes   **SERVES:** 4

150 ml (¼ pint) olive oil

350 g (11½ oz) cleaned squid, sliced into rings if large (see page 13)

8 large raw prawns, peeled and deveined

2 red or green peppers, deseeded and sliced

125 g (4 oz) piece chorizo sausage, diced

4 garlic cloves, crushed

1 onion, chopped

250 g (8 oz) paella rice

450 ml (¾ pint) Fish Stock (see page 17)

1 teaspoon saffron strands

100 g (3½ oz) peas

300–400 g (10–13 oz) mussels, cleaned (see page 12)

salt and pepper

lemon wedges, to serve

1 Heat half the oil in a large paella or frying pan and fry the squid and prawns, stirring, for 5 minutes. Drain with a slotted spoon. Add the peppers and fry for a further 5 minutes. Drain.

2 Add the chorizo, garlic, onion and remaining oil to the pan and fry for 5 minutes. Sprinkle in the rice and cook for 1 minute, stirring so that the grains become coated in the spicy oil.

3 Stir in the stock and saffron and bring to the boil. Reduce the heat, cover with a lid or foil and cook gently for about 20 minutes or until the rice is cooked through. Stir in the peas, along with the squid, prawns and peppers.

4 Push the mussels into the rice so that they are half submerged. Cover and cook for 3–4 minutes or until the mussels have opened. Discard any that remain closed. Season and serve with lemon wedges.

Chermoula-crusted shark

Chermoula is a hot, spicy, North African mixture that includes garlic, cumin, coriander and chilli. This version also uses peanuts and raisins, which complement the spices with their sweet, salty flavours.

PREPARATION TIME: 15 minutes, plus marinating
COOKING TIME: 20 minutes   **SERVES:** 4

4 tablespoons olive oil
finely grated rind and juice of 1 lemon
2 garlic cloves, crushed
½ teaspoon dried chilli flakes
4 shark steaks, each about 200 g (7 oz)
65 g (2½ oz) salted peanuts
15 g (½ oz) fresh coriander
2 tablespoons raisins
1 teaspoon cumin seeds, crushed

1 Mix together 2 tablespoons of the oil, the lemon rind and juice, garlic and chilli flakes. Put the shark steaks in a shallow baking dish and spoon over the oil mixture. Cover and leave to marinate for about 30 minutes.

2 Blend the peanuts and coriander in a food processor until coarsely chopped. Add the raisins and blend for a few seconds more.

3 Tip the mixture into a bowl and stir in the remaining oil and cumin seeds.

4 Uncover the shark steaks and bake in a preheated oven, 190°C (375°F), Gas Mark 5, for 10 minutes. Spread the steaks with the chermoula mixture, return to the oven and bake for a further 10 minutes or until the steaks are cooked through.

Swordfish confit

Once it is steeped in olive oil, the swordfish will keep well in the refrigerator overnight, making it a good menu choice if you've had to shop a day in advance. Try with other firm, meaty fish, such as shark or tuna. Let the leftover oil settle in a jug so you can strain it off, chill and use it in fish dishes for up to three days.

PREPARATION TIME: 10 minutes, plus chilling

COOKING TIME: 35 minutes   **SERVES:** 4

2 teaspoons chopped thyme

3 garlic cloves, crushed

½ teaspoon sea salt

¼ teaspoon crushed dried chilli flakes

4 swordfish steaks, skinned

150–200 ml (5–7 fl oz) olive oil

2 tablespoons lemon juice

4 tablespoons finely chopped parsley

1 tablespoon light muscovado sugar

1 tablespoon vodka

1 Mix together the thyme, garlic, salt and chilli flakes and rub the mixture all over the fish steaks.

2 Place the fish in a single layer in a shallow, ovenproof dish into which the pieces of fish fit snugly. Pour over enough oil to just cover the fish. (If the dish is too large, line it with foil, arrange the fish and bring the foil up around the fish so that you do not waste too much oil.) Cover and chill for up to 24 hours.

3 Bake in a preheated oven, 180°C, (350°F), Gas Mark 4, for 30 minutes or until the fish is cooked through.

4 Using a slotted spoon, drain the fish to serving plates. Mix together the lemon juice, parsley, sugar and vodka with 4 tablespoons of the cooking juices in a small saucepan. Whisk well, reheating gently, and spoon over the fish to serve.

Tuna Wellington

A good-sized piece of tuna, about 20 x 8.5 cm (8 x 3½ inches), is ideal for this dish. If you buy a fillet that's very chunky at one end, trim off the excess and grill or fry it for flaking into salads.

PREPARATION TIME: 30 minutes, plus cooling

COOKING TIME: 40 minutes   **SERVES:** 6

1 kg (2 lb) piece fresh tuna

50 g (2 oz) butter

1 shallot, finely chopped

350 g (11½ oz) mushrooms, roughly chopped

2 tablespoons hot horseradish sauce

3 tablespoons chopped tarragon

400 g (13 oz) puff pastry (thawed if frozen)

beaten egg, to glaze

salt and pepper

1 Pat the tuna dry on kitchen paper and rub all over with salt and pepper. Melt a knob of the butter in a frying pan and sear the tuna on all sides until browned. Drain and leave to cool.

2 Add half the remaining butter to the pan and gently fry the shallot and mushrooms until browned and all the moisture has evaporated. Stir in the horseradish sauce and tarragon and leave to cool. Spread the remaining butter over the tuna.

3 Roll out the pastry on a lightly floured surface to a large rectangle. Press half the mushroom mixture over the top of the tuna with your hands. Invert on to the pastry and spread with the remaining mushroom mixture.

4 Brush the pastry with beaten egg and bring it up over the tuna to enclose the fish completely, trimming off any bulky areas. Place the parcel, join side down, on a lightly greased baking sheet and brush with more egg. Bake in a preheated oven, 200°C (400°F), Gas Mark 6, for 30 minutes or until deep golden.

Tuna Wellington

Tuna and garlic mushroom skewers

For this recipe you'll need sturdy rosemary stalks to use as skewers. If you haven't got any in the garden (or can't buy any), use wooden or metal skewers instead and add a teaspoon of chopped rosemary to the garlic dressing.

PREPARATION TIME: 30 minutes

COOKING TIME: 10 minutes   **SERVES:** 4

500 g (1 lb) piece tuna

150 g (5 oz) piece baguette

200 g (7 oz) large chestnut mushrooms

4 stalks of rosemary, each 30 cm (12 inches) long

2 garlic cloves, crushed

1 teaspoon grainy mustard

8 tablespoons olive oil

salt and pepper

Roasted Tomato Sauce (see page 21), to serve

1 Cut the tuna into chunky slices, about 3.5 cm (1½ inches) thick. Cut each slice into 3.5 cm (1½ inch) squares. Tear the bread into pieces of a similar size. Blanch the mushrooms in boiling water for 1 minute. Drain.

2 Snip off most of the small stalks and leaves from the rosemary and cut off the stalk end at a slant to make threading easier. Carefully thread the tuna, bread and mushrooms on to the rosemary stalks. Place on a foil-lined grill rack.

3 Mix the garlic with the mustard, oil and a little seasoning and brush a little over the skewers.

4 Cook under a preheated moderate grill for 8–10 minutes, turning the skewers frequently and brushing with more of the garlic dressing. Serve the skewers with the tomato sauce.

Malaysian fish curry

Asian curries are quick to cook yet have a wonderfully full, fresh flavour. Swordfish works well as it doesn't fall apart during cooking. If you use one of the softer-fleshed, flakier white fish instead, reduce the cooking time and keep it in very big chunks.

PREPARATION TIME: 20 minutes

COOKING TIME: 20 minutes   **SERVES:** 4

750 g (1½ lb) swordfish steaks

3 shallots

2 garlic cloves, thinly sliced

15 g (½ oz) fresh root ginger, chopped

¼ teaspoon ground turmeric

1 red chilli, deseeded and chopped

400 ml (14 fl oz) can coconut milk

6 curry leaves

2 teaspoons palm or caster sugar

3 tablespoons vegetable oil

1 tablespoon coriander seeds, crushed

2 teaspoons cumin seeds, crushed

2 teaspoons fennel seeds, crushed

15 g (½ oz) fresh coriander, chopped

salt and pepper

1 Cut the swordfish steaks into chunky pieces, discarding the skin and any bones. Season with salt and pepper.

2 Roughly chop 2 of the shallots and put them in a food processor with 1 garlic clove, the ginger, turmeric, chilli and 2 tablespoons of the coconut milk. Blend to a smooth paste, scraping the mixture down from the side of the bowl.

3 Scrape the paste into a large saucepan and add the remaining coconut milk, curry leaves and sugar. Bring to the boil, then reduce the heat and simmer gently for 5 minutes. Lower in the fish and cook gently for a further 10 minutes.

4 Finely slice the remaining shallot. Heat the oil in a small frying pan. Add the shallot, the remaining garlic and cumin and fennel seeds and fry gently for 3 minutes. Stir in the coriander, spoon over the curry and serve.

Oven-steamed salmon with Asian greens
Oven-steaming fish is pretty effortless – just make sure that you have a rack that sits at least 1 cm (½ inch) above the base of the tin.

PREPARATION TIME: 15 minutes

COOKING TIME: 25 minutes   **SERVES:** 4

4 chunky salmon steaks, each about 200 g (7 oz)

1 tablespoon tamarind paste

2–3 tablespoons soy sauce

15 g (½ oz) fresh root ginger, grated

2 teaspoons caster sugar

2 garlic cloves, crushed

1 mild green chilli, finely sliced

1 teaspoon cornflour

250 g (8 oz) pak choi

8 spring onions, halved lengthways

15 g (½ oz) fresh coriander, chopped

1 Put the salmon steaks on an oiled roasting rack or wire rack inside a roasting tin and pour 450 ml (¾ pint) boiling water into the tin. Cover tightly with foil and cook in a preheated oven, 180°C (350°F), Gas Mark 4, for 15 minutes or until the salmon is almost cooked through.

2 Meanwhile, put the tamarind in a small saucepan and blend in 175 ml (6 fl oz) water. Stir in the soy sauce, ginger, sugar, garlic and chilli and heat through gently for 5 minutes. Blend the cornflour with 1 tablespoon water and add to the pan. Heat gently, stirring, for 1–2 minutes or until thickened.

3 Quarter the pak choi lengthways into wedges and arrange the pieces around the salmon on the rack with the spring onions. Re-cover and return to the oven for a further 8–10 minutes or until the vegetables have wilted.

4 Stir the coriander into the sauce. Transfer the fish and greens to warm serving plates, pour over the sauce and serve.

Oven-steamed salmon with Asian greens

Sugar and spice salmon
Get the oven really hot before you start cooking this sizzling supper dish. It's got more than enough flavour to serve on its own, but if you want a contrasting sauce, try the Crème Fraîche and Herb Mayonnaise on page 20.

PREPARATION TIME: 5 minutes

COOKING TIME: 10 minutes   SERVES: 4

4 salmon fillets, each about 200 g (7 oz)

3 tablespoons light muscovado sugar

2 garlic cloves, crushed

1 teaspoon cumin seeds, crushed

1 teaspoon smoked or ordinary paprika

1 tablespoon white wine vinegar

2 tablespoons groundnut oil

salt

lemon or lime wedges, to serve

1 Put the salmon fillets in a lightly oiled roasting tin. Mix together the sugar, garlic, cumin seeds, paprika, vinegar and a little salt.

2 Using a dessertspoon, spread the mixture all over the fish so that it is thinly coated. Drizzle with the oil.

3 Bake in a preheated oven, 220°C (425°F), Gas Mark 7, for 10 minutes or until the fish is cooked through. Transfer to warm serving plates and serve garnished with lemon or lime wedges.

Salmon and crab fishcakes
Some fish recipes are best left quite simple, letting a few quality ingredients speak for themselves. Leave out the crabmeat and add an extra potato for an everyday version.

PREPARATION TIME: 25 minutes
COOKING TIME: 30 minutes   **SERVES:** 4

700 g (1 lb 7 oz) baking potatoes

350 g (11½ oz) skinned salmon fillet

4 tablespoons milk

25 g (1 oz) butter

150 g (5 oz) dressed crabmeat

2 tablespoons chopped tarragon

2 tablespoons chopped parsley

2 tablespoons capers, rinsed and drained

1 egg, beaten

flour, for dusting

mild olive oil, for shallow-frying

salt and pepper

Crème Fraîche and Herb Mayonnaise (see page 20), to
  serve

1 Cook the potatoes in plenty of lightly salted boiling water for about 15 minutes or until tender. Meanwhile, put the salmon in a frying pan, pour over the milk, cover and cook gently for 8–10 minutes or until cooked through.

2 Drain the potatoes and return to the pan. Use a potato masher to crush the potatoes, leaving them in slightly chunky pieces. Stir in the butter.

3 When it is cool enough to handle, flake the salmon into chunky pieces, reserving the pan juices and checking for any bones. Add the fish and pan juices to the potatoes with the crabmeat, herbs, capers, beaten egg and a little seasoning. Beat well until combined.

4 Using well-floured hands, shape into 8 equal balls, packing the mixture firmly together, then flatten into cakes. Heat a thin layer of oil in a heavy-based frying pan and fry the cakes, half at a time, for about 3 minutes on each side until golden. Serve hot with the mayonnaise.

Perch fritters with lime and sage butter
Perch is one of the tastiest of the river fish, but it must be scaled, gutted and eaten while it's really fresh. Like most river catches, perch is only fleetingly available, but salmon or trout make good substitutes.

PREPARATION TIME: 30 minutes

COOKING TIME: 10 minutes   **SERVES:** 4

1 lime

50 g (2 oz) butter

2 tablespoons olive oil

12 sage leaves, shredded

1 red shallot or small red onion, finely chopped

8 perch fillets

flour, for dusting

1 egg, lightly beaten

100 g (3½ oz) breadcrumbs

vegetable oil, for frying

salt and pepper

1 Halve the lime lengthways and thinly slice each half. Melt 15 g (½ oz) of the butter in a small saucepan with the olive oil until bubbling. Add the sage leaves and fry for 15 seconds. Drain the sage with a slotted spoon, add the shallot or onion to the pan and fry gently for 2 minutes. Remove from the heat and add the remaining butter, sage leaves, lime slices, a little salt and plenty of pepper. Leave to stand while you cook the fish.

2 Cut the perch into chunks. Season the flour on a plate and use it to dust the fish. Coat the fish in beaten egg, then in the breadcrumbs.

3 Add vegetable oil to a depth of 1.5 cm (¾ inch) in a large frying pan and heat until a few breadcrumbs sizzle and turn golden in 30 seconds. Lower half the pieces of fish into the pan and fry until golden, turning once. Drain on kitchen paper while you fry the remainder.

4 Reheat the lime and sage butter and spoon over the cooked fritters to serve.

Baked stuffed trout

Like all river-caught fish, trout needs to be served very fresh and with plenty of interesting flavours to perk up its tendency towards earthiness. This idea adapts well to most edible river fish, so it's a useful recipe if you are presented with the catch of a successful day's fishing. Serve with chips or creamy mash.

PREPARATION TIME: 15 minutes

COOKING TIME: 35 minutes   **SERVES:** 2

2 small trout, cleaned

25 g (1 oz) butter, plus extra to grease

1 onion, chopped

1 tablespoon chopped lemon thyme

2 teaspoons hot horseradish sauce

1 garlic clove, crushed

50 g (2 oz) breadcrumbs

1 glass white wine

salt and pepper

1 Score the trout several times down each side and arrange them, side by side, in a small, shallow, buttered ovenproof dish.

2 Melt the butter in a frying pan and gently fry the onion for 5 minutes. Add the thyme, horseradish, garlic and breadcrumbs and fry gently, stirring, for 2 minutes.

3 Season the stuffing to taste and pack it into the fish cavities. Pour over the wine and cover the dish with buttered greaseproof paper.

4 Bake in a preheated oven, 180°C (350°F), Gas Mark 4, for 25–30 minutes or until the fish is cooked through.

Smoked and preserved fish

Before refrigeration was available, fish was smoked, pickled or salted so that it could be eaten all year round. The recipes that include this type of fish tend, therefore, to be traditional, well-loved dishes, such as kedgeree and brandade. Smoked fish also makes delicious pâtés and is an ideal and flavourful ingredient for featuring in fresh summer salads.

Escabèche

There are many variations on the theme of steeping lightly cooked fish in seasoned, sweetened vinegar. This delicious version is made with succulent pieces of chunky cod.

PREPARATION TIME: 15 minutes, plus chilling

COOKING TIME: 10 minutes   **SERVES:** 4

500 g (1 lb) cod fillet, skinned
4 tablespoons olive oil
1 pointed red pepper, deseeded and thinly sliced
1 red onion, thinly sliced
2 pared strips orange rind, plus 2 tablespoons juice
½ teaspoon cumin seeds, crushed
good pinch of ground turmeric
125 ml (4 fl oz) sherry vinegar
5 tablespoons light muscovado sugar
8 pitted green olives
salt and pepper

1 Cut the cod into chunky pieces, discarding any stray bones, and season lightly with salt and pepper.

2 Heat the oil in a frying pan and gently fry the fish on both sides for about 5 minutes or until just cooked through. Drain to a non-metallic dish in which the pieces fit quite snugly. Gently fry the red pepper and onion in the pan until softened and add them to the dish.

3 Tuck the orange rind between the pieces of fish. Mix together the orange juice, cumin seeds, turmeric, vinegar and sugar until the sugar has dissolved, then pour the mixture over the fish.

4 Turn the ingredients gently to combine. Cover and chill for up to 3 days.

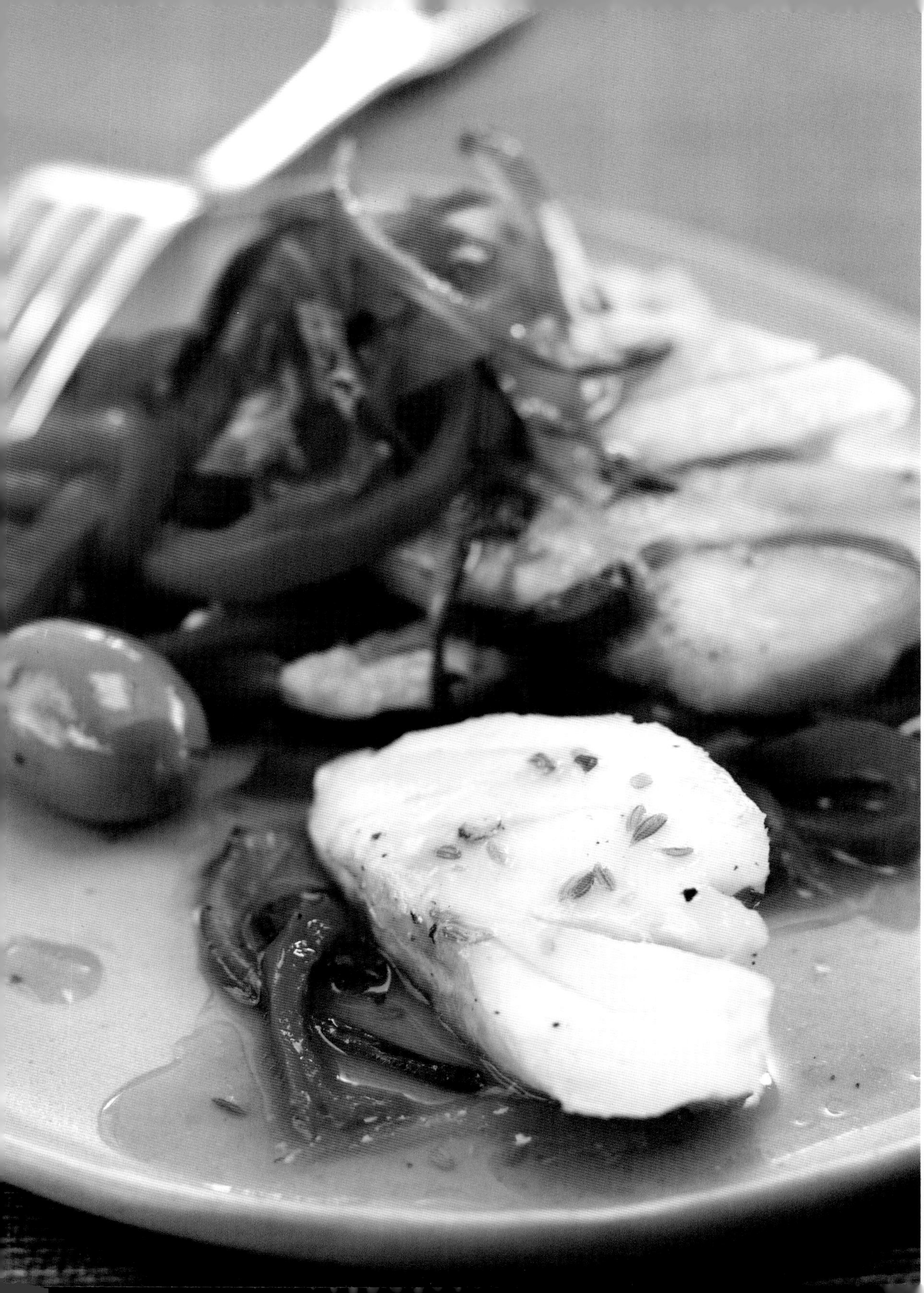

Escabèche

Salt cod fritters

Allow a good two to three days' soaking time to soften and remove the saltiness from the cod before making these delicious little fritters. They're usually served 'tapas style' with drinks and a little bowl of aïoli for dipping.

PREPARATION TIME: 20 minutes, plus soaking and standing

COOKING TIME: 30 minutes   SERVES: 4–6

350 g (11½ oz) salt cod, soaked for 48–72 hours (see page 11)

125 g (4 oz) plain flour

2 tablespoons olive oil

1 egg white

vegetable oil, for frying

Aïoli (see page 20), to serve

1 Drain the soaked cod and put it in a saucepan with enough fresh water to cover. Bring to a simmer and cook gently for about 20 minutes or until the fish is tender. Drain, and when it is cool enough to handle, discard the skin and any bones. Leave to cool.

2 Make the batter. Put the flour in a bowl, making a well in the centre. Pour in the olive oil and 150 ml (¼ pint) water. Whisk the liquid, gradually incorporating the flour, to make a smooth paste. Leave to stand for 30 minutes.

3 Meanwhile, cut the cod into 1–1.5 cm (½–¾ inch) chunks. The fish may well fall into flaky chunks rather that neat cubes, which is perfectly acceptable.

4 Whisk the egg white until peaking and fold it into the batter. Add vegetable oil to a depth of 5 cm (2 inches) to a large saucepan and heat until a drop of the batter sizzles and turns golden in about 30 seconds.

5 Dip the cod in the batter and lower into the oil. Add several more pieces and fry gently for about 2 minutes or until they are puffed and golden. Drain on crumpled kitchen paper and keep warm while you cook the remainder. Serve with the Aïoli.

Brandade

A well-loved dish in Provence, this is a smooth, creamy blend of salt cod, olive oil and cream, whipped to a fluffy, mousse-like consistency. Serve as a lovely, summery snack or starter, or scooped on to toast as a nibble with drinks.

PREPARATION TIME: 10 minutes, plus soaking

COOKING TIME: 20 minutes   **SERVES**: 6–8

700 g (1 lb 7 oz) salt cod, soaked for 48–72 hours (see page 11)

2 bay leaves

1 onion, quartered

300 ml (½ pint) single cream

200 ml (7 fl oz) olive oil

2 garlic cloves, crushed

squeeze of lemon juice

pepper

chopped parsley, to garnish

toasted baguette, to serve

1 Drain the soaked cod and put it in a saucepan with enough fresh water to cover. Add the bay leaves and onion and bring to a simmer. Cook gently for about 20 minutes or until very tender. Drain the fish, and when it is cool enough to handle, discard the skin and any bones.

2 Put the cream and oil in a saucepan and heat gently, whisking occasionally, until hot and bubbling.

3 Put the cod and garlic in a food processor and blend until smooth, gradually adding the cream and oil mixture until it forms a pale, smooth purée. Blend in the lemon juice and pepper to taste.

4 Transfer to a serving dish and sprinkle with parsley. Serve with toasted baguette for scooping up the brandade.

Smoked haddock crêpes

Succulent pieces of fish, bathed in a creamy cheese sauce and rolled up in pancakes, make a comforting supper dish. If you prefer, use firm-fleshed, unsmoked white fish instead.

PREPARATION TIME: 40 minutes

COOKING TIME: 50 minutes   **SERVES:** 4

125 g (4 oz) plain flour

1 egg

300 ml (½ pint) milk, plus 4 tablespoons

450 g (14½ oz) undyed smoked haddock

groundnut oil, for shallow-frying

200 g (7 oz) baby spinach

Rich Cheese Sauce (see page 18)

25 g (1 oz) Parmesan cheese, grated

salt and pepper

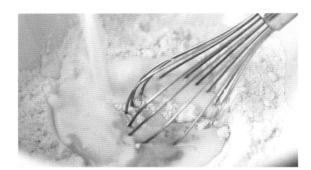

1 Whisk the flour, egg and 150 ml (¼ pint) of the milk in a bowl until it is smooth. Whisk in another 150 ml (¼ pint) milk.

2 Cook the haddock in the 4 tablespoons milk in a frying pan, covered, for 8–10 minutes. Leave to cool.

3 Heat a little oil in a crêpe pan until it begins to smoke. Pour off the excess and pour a little batter into the pan, tilting it to coat the base. Cook until the edges curl and the crêpe is cooked on the underside. Flip over and cook the other side briefly. Slide on to a plate and cook the remainder in the same way.

4 Wilt the spinach in a covered saucepan with 1 tablespoon water. Drain. Flake the fish, discarding the skin and any bones. Reserve one-third of the cheese sauce and stir the fish into the remainder.

5 Scatter each crêpe with spinach, spoon a little of the fish and sauce down the centre and season lightly. Roll up and arrange in a line in a shallow, ovenproof dish. Spoon over the remaining sauce and sprinkle with the grated Parmesan. Bake in a preheated oven, 190°C (375°F), Gas Mark 5, for 20–25 minutes.

Smoked mackerel pâté

This pâté is infinitely versatile. You can swap the mackerel for other preserved fish, such as smoked trout, salmon or eel, or even canned sardines. Whizzed up to a creamy consistency in a food processor, it's a good choice if you need to make a snack or starter at short notice.

PREPARATION TIME: 5 minutes

SERVES: 4–6

300 g (10 oz) smoked mackerel

2 teaspoons pink or green peppercorns in brine, rinsed and drained

25 g (1 oz) butter, melted

2 tablespoons lime juice

200 g (7 oz) cream cheese

salt

lumpfish roe, to garnish (optional)

watercress and toast, to serve

1 Skin the fish and flake into a food processor. Add the peppercorns and blend to a smooth paste.

2 Add the butter, lime juice and cream cheese and blend until thick and creamy, scraping the mixture down from the side of the bowl if necessary.

3 Check the seasoning and spoon into a serving bowl or little individual dishes. Scatter with lumpfish roe (if used) and serve with watercress and toast.

Dill-pickled salmon

In this well-loved Scandinavian dish, salmon is pickled in a delicious, sweet dill marinade. Allow two or three days for making the salmon and serve as a starter or lunch dish with rye or granary bread.

PREPARATION TIME: 20 minutes, plus marinating
SERVES: 8–10

2 middle-cut salmon fillets, each about 500 g (1 lb), scaled and boned
25 g (1 oz) chopped dill
40 g (1½ oz) coarse sea salt
50 g (2 oz) caster sugar
2 tablespoons black peppercorns, crushed
Sauce:
2 tablespoons French brown mustard
4 teaspoons caster sugar
4 tablespoons chopped dill
100 ml (3½ fl oz) Mayonnaise (see page 20)

1 Lay one salmon fillet, skin side down, in a shallow, non-metallic dish. Mix together the dill, salt, sugar and peppercorns and scatter over the fish. Cover with the second piece of fish, skin side up.

2 Cover the dish with foil, place a small tray or plate over it and balance several kitchen weights or full cans on top. Chill for 48–72 hours, turning the fish over once or twice a day and spooning the juices that seep out over the fish.

3 To make the sauce, beat together all the ingredients and put the mixture in a small serving dish.

4 To serve, drain one salmon fillet to a chopping board. Using a very sharp knife, cut off thin, slanting slices, not much thicker than smoked salmon. Serve with the sauce.

Kipper kedgeree

Although it is usually made with smoked haddock, kedgeree adapts well to almost any smoked fish, so look out for the best deal when you are shopping.

PREPARATION TIME: 15 minutes

COOKING TIME: 15 minutes   **SERVES:** 4

250 g (8 oz) basmati rice

4 eggs

625 g (1¼ lb) kippers

2 teaspoons fennel seeds

8 cardamom pods

65 g (2½ oz) butter

1 onion, finely chopped

1 teaspoon ground turmeric

1 cinnamon stick

4 tablespoons chopped parsley

salt and pepper

lemon or lime wedges, to serve

1 Cook the rice in plenty of boiling water for about 10 minutes or until tender. Put the eggs in a separate saucepan, cover with freshly boiled water and bring to the boil. Simmer gently for 5 minutes. Drain the rice and eggs.

2 Meanwhile, put the kippers in a frying pan, just cover with hot water and simmer gently for 5 minutes. Drain. When the fish is cool enough to handle, roughly flake the flesh, discarding the skin and bones. Shell and quarter the boiled eggs.

3 Use a pestle and mortar to crush the fennel seeds and cardamom pods. Remove the cardamom pods, leaving the seeds.

4 Melt half the butter in a frying pan and gently fry the onion and all the spices for 5 minutes. Stir in the rice, fish, eggs and parsley and season to taste. Serve with lemon or lime wedges.

Smoked trout with pickled cucumber
This perfect combination of flavours is easy to put together, particularly if you like 'make-ahead' dishes. It's great for a leisurely lunch or a light starter when there's plenty to follow.

PREPARATION TIME: 10 minutes, plus standing

SERVES: 4

1 medium cucumber, about 500 g (1 lb)

2 teaspoons salt

2 tablespoons caster sugar

4 tablespoons white wine vinegar

3 tablespoons chopped dill or tarragon

250 g (8 oz) smoked trout fillet

2 spring onions, finely sliced

pepper

1 Peel the cucumber and thinly slice. Layer the slices in a colander, adding a sprinkling of salt after every few layers. Leave to stand for 30 minutes.

2 Plunge the colander into cold water to remove the salt and leave to drain completely. Mix together the sugar, vinegar and dill or tarragon.

3 Toss the cucumber in the herb mixture and chill until ready to serve.

4 Pile the cucumber salad on to serving plates. Break the trout fillets into large pieces and scatter them over the top with the spring onions. Season lightly with black pepper and serve.

Marinated herring and haricot bean salad *This is a good snack or starter to make when you see really fresh, plump herrings. Immersed in a tangy marinade that helps preserve the fish, this will keep well in the refrigerator for up to three days.*

PREPARATION TIME: 10 minutes, plus cooling
COOKING TIME: 3 minutes   **SERVES:** 4

4 herrings, filleted

200 ml (7 fl oz) cider vinegar

2 teaspoons sea salt

4 tablespoons caster sugar

1 teaspoon coriander seeds, crushed

1 teaspoon mustard seeds, crushed

pinch of ground allspice

2 bay leaves

2 salad onions or 4 spring onions, shredded

410 g (13½ oz) can haricot beans, rinsed and drained

4 tablespoons chopped parsley

1 tablespoon chopped mint

crusty bread to serve

1 Cut each herring fillet in half and scatter in a shallow, non-metallic dish.

2 Put the vinegar, salt, sugar, spices and bay leaves in a saucepan and bring just to the boil, stirring until the sugar has dissolved. Pour the marinade over the fish and leave it to cool completely.

3 Stir in the salad or spring onions, beans, parsley and mint. Cover and chill for up to 3 days. Serve with crusty bread for mopping up the juices.

Index

Acknowledgements

Photography: © Octopus Publishing Group Ltd / Stephen Conroy

Executive Editor Sarah Ford
Editor Emma Pattison
Executive Art Editor Penny Stock
Design Geoff Borin
Senior Production Controller Martin Croshaw
Photographer Stephen Conroy
Food Stylist Joanna Farrow
Props Stylist Liz Hippisley